Lightweight Expeditions

LIGHTWEIGHT
EXPEDITIONS

Rob Collister

The Crowood Press

First published in 1989 by
The Crowood Press
Ramsbury, Marlborough
Wiltshire SN8 2HE

British Library Cataloguing in Publication Data

Collister, Rob
  Lightweight expeditions.
  1. Lightweight mountaineering expeditions
  I. Title
  910′.09143

  ISBN 1 85223 139 4

Picture Credits
All colour photographs by Rob Collister
Black and white photographs by Rob Collister, David Williams
(Figs 13, 16, 82), Alun Hughes (Fig 4), Des Rubens (Fig 53), and
Simon Brown (Fig 104).

Typeset by Photosetting, Yeovil
Printed in Great Britain by The Bath Press

Contents

Acknowledgements

My grateful thanks to: John Cousins, Doug Wilson, Ann Mitcalfe, Les Harvey and Chris Bulstrode for helpful comment and advice; David Williams, Alun Hughes, Des Rubens, Simon Brown and Dick Isherwood for photographs; Steve Cone for help producing negatives from transparencies; Dave Alcock and Derek Mayes of Plas y Brenin and Tony Schärer of Rhyd y Creuau for the use of their darkrooms; Sue and Ron Bury for typing and photocopying; Ross and Astrid Clapcott and Grant Harvey for repeatedly crossing the Tongariro river in midwinter for the camera; and Netti, my wife, who crossed the river too, toned down some of my remarks, read the proofs, compiled the index and has been as cheerful and encouraging during the writing of this book as she has been on many a mountain adventure; also my son, Daniel, who drew the diagrams and the cartoon.

Introduction

This book is not intended for old hands who will know it all; nor is it intended for newcomers to the mountains. It is aimed at experienced mountaineers who have climbed on both rock and on ice in Britain or the United States, and have had at least two seasons of alpine climbing, who want to apply their skills in a remoter setting or on higher mountains. Therefore, there is no discussion of climbing technique, ropework, crevasse rescue or avalanches, all important topics but covered elsewhere in textbooks on ice-climbing or alpinism. In fact, with the exception of the section on river-crossing, there are no skills to be taught, so this is not so much a textbook as a compendium of suggestions and advice. On some topics I have offered opinions that may be controversial, but I think I have made it clear that they *are* only opinions. There are no rules in mountaineering.

I strongly recommend that no one is in such a hurry to visit the greater ranges that he or she leaves out an alpine apprenticeship. Before my first trip to the Himalaya I had only one alpine season under my belt, and that a short and not very successful one. My companions, although older, were not as experienced as I assumed. We learned far too many basic lessons the hard way. For instance, two of us ploughed up a steep, narrow couloir in the middle of the afternoon and escaped being wiped out by stonefall by a hair's breadth. It was a foolish place to be at that time of day.

Two days later we were descending a remote glacier, three days from base camp. I jumped an obvious snow-bridge cutting across the dry-ice glacier. Assuming Alan had seen me, I said nothing and did not even glance behind me. Seconds later the rope to my waist jerked tight, pulling me to the ground. Braking desperately with the pick of my axe, I was dragged backwards towards the crevasse. Only a constriction in which Alan wedged thirty feet down saved me from joining him in the depths – probably for ever. We had no ice-screws, curved picks had not been invented and I had never heard of an ice-bollard. The ice was far too hard for either pick or spike of my axe to penetrate. All I could do was pass the rope round the shaft of my axe, support it with my leg and hope for the best. At Alan's first attempt to prusik out, this inadequate belay, not surprisingly, collapsed. I arranged my body in a stronger position to prop up the axe but it took Alan half an hour to appear at the surface. By that time he was totally exhausted and unable to pull himself over the lip. Ten feet away I could do nothing to help and had such agonizing cramp in my leg that I could not have held Alan's weight much longer. Finally, he constructed an etrier out of his prusik loops to gain a little extra height and scrabbled over the edge. It was a near thing; and from start to finish demonstrated our lack of experience.

After that, we had numerous other minor epics but we went on to climb five new peaks between four of us. I would not have missed the experience for anything, but in retrospect I think I, for one, should not have been there – my first expedition was too nearly my last. Both episodes were the

Fig 2   Alan Cormack beside the crevasse that swallowed him up, with the improvised etrier that enabled him to escape.

result of elementary mistakes and a lack of knowledge that could easily have been acquired in the Alps, where there is no shortage of people to offer advice.

DEFINITIONS

I had better come clean right at the start and admit that the title *Lightweight Expeditions* is a misnomer. It is a convenient peg to hang the book on, as the term is in common usage and everybody has a rough idea what it means. But I am not really writing about expeditions and 'lightweight' means anything but a light weight on your back. An expedition implies a lot of people, with a lot of baggage, spending a lot of money (prefer-

ably not their own); whereas I have in mind a small group, with not much more baggage than they can carry themselves, on a climbing holiday costing no more than they could reasonably expect to save in a year if they had a job and not too large a mortgage. However, for convenience I have stayed with the term 'expedition'.

For the purpose of this book, the climbing does not have to be in the Himalaya or Greenland: it can be anywhere more than a day's journey from a road and where there is no infrastructure of huts and made paths, or at a higher altitude than the Alps. What do I mean by 'lightweight'? My meaning becomes clear in the text, but to attempt a complicated, all-embracing definition would, I think, be a waste of time. I prefer to think of it as an attitude of mind that regards the process as more important than the goal; that prefers to be free from external pressures and obligations to succeed, yet accepts the responsibility to make a minimal impact on the mountain environment. The end does not necessarily justify all the means that may be available. To climb a mountain without the help of fixed rope, radios or Sherpas is, I believe, not only cheaper and easier to organize, but infinitely more rewarding in personal terms. This is not to say that there is no satisfaction in a big expedition, only that there is more in a small one.

We all go to the hills for different reasons. For many, the climb and the reaching of a summit are important aspects of an expedition – they are a focus and a climax – but they are not the be-all and end-all of it. Equally important are the journey to it and the living in wild, empty mountains. To stand upon a virgin summit knowing that there is not a soul within fifty miles is a marvellous feeling. To share a base camp or a route with several other groups (as seems to be increasingly the case in Nepal, the Karakoram and the Andes), sadly diminishes the experience of a climb, as it does in the Alps, too. The climb is still there, good fellowship may be there, but not wilderness. I realize that some climbers do not share this feeling, in fact, regard it as a nonsense; but the beauty of the lightweight

Fig 3   Netti Collister on a summit in Kishtwar, a long way from anywhere or anyone.

11

approach is that it gives you the flexibility to change objective, to get off the beaten track and savour wilderness, if you wish.

I am aware of a contradiction in loving empty mountains and writing a book encouraging people into the empty places that are left. My only defence is that numbers are less critical than attitudes. The important thing is not how many people have visited an area, or are visiting it, but how they behave and what they leave behind; in other words, the extent to which they impinge on each other's consciousness. Wilderness, like beauty, is an experience in people, rather than an objective reality, and as such it is easily damaged by another's thoughtlessness. I can still feel the stab of disappointment at finding a plastic detergent bottle washed up on the beach of a lonely fiord in Greenland fifteen years ago. If this book encourages climbers not just to go on expeditions, but to move 'on soft foot' through the mountains, then it has been worth writing.

WHAT'S NEW?

People sometimes assume that lightweight expeditions are something new. Nothing could be further from the truth. When Mummery went to Nanga Parbat in 1895 he assumed that he could climb it exactly like an alpine peak. He underestimated the scale of the mountain and the effects of altitude, but there have been many others since then

Fig 4   A horseman saddles up in the Yarkhun valley which divides the Hindu Kush from the Hindu Raj mountains.

*Fig 5   A jeep on the Lowari pass between Dir and Chitral in
northern Pakistan.*

who have sought to emulate his approach. The heavyweight expeditions to Everest in the 1920s and 1930s established a format which was carried over into the so-called 'golden age' of the 1950s and 1960s and has been imitated on much lower peaks worldwide ever since. But both before and after the Everest mentality took a grip on expeditions in general, some very bold unsupported climbing was accomplished.

In 1905 Tom Longstaff, with the Brocherel brothers Henri and Alexis from Courmayeur, made an attempt on Gurla Mandhata in Tibet (a mountain which is still unclimbed). Their expedition has a very modern ring to it. Leaving their tent and sleeping bags at about 5,900 metres they set off with food for two days. Descending off the West Ridge at about 7,000 metres to look for a bivi-site, they were all swept down 900 metres by a wet-snow avalanche. Undaunted, they bivouacked where they were and next day continued upwards by a different route. At about 7,000 metres they stopped early, suffering from headaches, and Henri enlarged a small crevasse into a snow cave.

'That night dinner had to be dispensed with. I coiled down the silk rope on the icy floor, wrapped my putties loosely round my legs and thrust my feet into my rucksack. I dreamed that Sherring had sent a square khaki-coloured water-cart full of warm wraps up the glacier to us, but when it arrived it contained only Jaeger stockings and the driver, in spite of my violent abuse, insisted that we were only entitled to one pair each. Hence I was so cold that I roused up the men at two o'clock.'

This My Voyage (John Murray 1950)

Sadly, they were stopped by a bergschrund at 7,300 metres and were unable to find a way across in the dark. Longstaff became so cold that, rather than wait for day-break, they decided to retreat. They were walking for another seventeen hours that day and it was yet another day before they had a square meal...

An empty stomach seems to be a common price to pay for a lightweight expedition. Shipton, Tilman and their three Sherpas were reduced to eating roots on their descent through the jungle from the Nanda Devi Sanctuary. The four months they spent in that area and Shipton's account of their explorations in *Nanda Devi* (Hodder and Stoughton 1936) epitomize all the trials and tribulations, uncertainties and excitements, joys and rewards of lightweight mountaineering. I can do no better than quote one of Shipton's closing paragraphs:

'The high mountains were now showing signs of approaching winter, a sharp reminder that our season of freedom and perfect happiness was at an end. But the marches which followed have left their quota of memories. A struggle to find an exit from the grim gorge in the upper Sunderdhunga Valley into which we had blundered in a heavy mist; our last encounter with a swollen mountain river; an enormous feast of wild raspberries and Himalayan blackberries further down the valley; the generous hospitality of the first villagers we met, and the sweetness of their honey; the sparkling sunlit mornings, as one lay, sleepily watching the smoke of a distant wood fire mounting straight up into the clear air; a dawn on the distant ice-clad giants, whose presence we had just left.'

1 Planning

Tilman – or was it Shipton? – declared somewhere that any expedition that could not be planned on the back of an envelope was too complicated to be worth the candle. Few of my own trips have been quite so simple, I have to admit, but there was one where planning amounted to no more than a postcard which read: 'How about Distaghil Sar? Buy a goat in Hispar and drive it up the glacier. See you in Rawalpindi. Dick.' In theory, once you know the ropes, it is perfectly possible to pack your rucksack, buy an air ticket and go climbing almost anywhere at the drop of a hat.

That is all very well if you have done it a few times. You will have a fair idea of what you want to climb, how to get there, what you will need in the way of visas and inoculations, if any, how much gear to take and so on. But if you have never travelled outside Europe (or the States), it will all be a big unknown and, if exciting, more than a little daunting too. It will pay to do your homework thoroughly before your first

Fig 6   It is not easy for a lightweight expedition to climb in Antarctica where this picture was taken, but similar mountains can be found and similar transport used in many parts of Greenland, Alaska and Arctic Canada.

Fig 7   Approaching the coast of East Greenland. Pack-ice is always a potential problem in Polar regions, even in summer.

trip; you can play it by ear later if you want to. This section is intended to be a starting point. It cannot provide all the answers, but it tells you where to look.

WHERE TO CLIMB

There is a tendency, certainly in Europe, to think of expeditions in terms of the Himalaya. This is not really surprising for it is relatively cheap to fly there and, taken in its general sense, the Himalaya is something like fifteen hundred miles long by two hundred wide, which adds up to a lot of mountains. Yet even within the Himalaya attention tends to be concentrated on a very

few peaks. Continental climbers especially seem to be obsessed by the figure '8,000' and current policy is to allow a free-for-all on the most sought-after peaks – except that they are not free. In Nepal, during the post-monsoon season of 1988, thirty-one expeditions out of a total of fifty were climbing on the country's eight 8,000-metre peaks.

It is easier, cheaper and more fun to climb on smaller mountains, of which there are huge numbers in other parts of the Himalaya, not to mention the rest of the world. The list that follows is far from exhaustive and is intended only to give an indication of the almost unlimited scope that exists for lightweight expedition mountaineering. Basically, the world's your oyster.

Country	Range or District	Highest Peak(s)
Afghanistan	Badakhshan	Koh-i-Bandaka
	Wakhan	Lunkho
Alaska	Brooks Range	Arrigetch peaks
	Alaska Range, west	McKinley, Foraker, Hunter
	Alaska Range, east	Deborah, Hayes, Hess
	Chugach Mountains	Thompson Ridge, Granite Range
	Wrangells	Sanford
	Glacier Bay	Fairweather
	Kitchatna Mountains	Cathedral Spires
Argentina	Patagonia	Fitzroy, Cerro Torre
Argentina/ Chile	Northern Andes	Cerro el Toro
	Central Andes	Aconcagua, Mercedario
Bhutan	Assam Himalaya	Chomolhari, Jicchu Drake
Bolivia	Cordillera Real	Illampu, Ancohuma
Canada	Ellesmere Island	
	Baffin Island	Asgard, Overlord
	Logan Mountains	Lotus-flower Tower
	St Elias Range	Logan, St Elias
	Coast Range	Waddington
Chad	Tibesti	Pic Tousside
Chile	Patagonia	Towers of Paine
	Tierra del Fuego	Darwin
China	Kun Lun	Xinging, Amne Machin
	South Xinjiang	Kongur, Mustagh Ata
	Tien Shan (east)	Bogda Shan
	Da Xue Shan	Minya Konka

(The northern side of the entire Himalayan chain also lies within one or other of the Chinese provinces.)

Country	Range or District	Highest Peak(s)
Colombia	Sierra Nevada de Santa Marta	Pico Simmons
	Cordillera Central	Tolima, Huila
	Cordillera Oriental	Ritacuba Blanca and Negra
Ecuador	Cordillera Occidental	Chimborazo, Cotopaxi
	Altar Range	
Ethiopia	Simien Mountains	Ras Dashen

Country	Range or District	Highest Peak(s)
Greenland	Peary Land	Roosevelt Range, Benedict Mnts
	Staunings Alps	Dansketinde
	Watkins Mountains	Gunnbjorn's Feld
	Angmassalik Area	Mount Forel, Ingolsfjeld
	South Coast	Tasermiut Fiord
	West Coast	Punta Italia
		Upernavik Island
Iceland	Vatnajökull	Hvannadol Shnjukur
India	Ladakh	Saser Kangri, Rimu
	Kashmir	Nun-Kun, Kolahoi
	Kishtwar	Sickle Moon, Brammah
	Lahul	Mulkila, White Sail
	Kulu	Deo Tibba, Indrasan
	Garwhal	Nanda Devi, Gangotri Glacier
	Sikkim	Kanchenjunga, Pauhunri
Indonesia	Carstensz Mountains	Carstensz Pyramid
Iran	Elburz Mountains	Damavand
	Zagros Mountains	Kuh-e-Denar
Kenya	Mount Kenya	Batian, Nelion
Morocco	High Atlas	Toukbal
Nepal	Karnali	Api, Nampa
	Dolpo	Kanjiroba
	Dhaulagiri Himal	Dhaulagiri I–VI
	Annapurna Himal	Annapurna I–IV
	Larkya Himal	Manaslu, Himalchuli
	Langtang Himal	Langtang Lirung
	Jugal Himal	Dorje Lakpa
	Rowaling	Gauri Sankar
	Sola Khumbu	Cho Oyu, Everest, Makalu
	Eastern border	Kanchenjunga
Norway	Lyngen Alps	Jiekevarri
	Spitzbergen	Newtontoppen

Country	Range or District	Highest Peak(s)
Pakistan	Chitral	Tirich Mir, Noshaq
	Hunza	Rakaposhi, Batura
	Nagar	Distaghil Sar, Trivor
	Baltistan	K2, Gasherbrum I–IV
	Chilas	Nanga Parbat
	Swat	Falak Sar
Peru	Cordillera Blanca	Huascaran, Huandoy
	Cordillera Huayhuash	Yerupaja, Siula Grande
	Cordillera Vilacambra	Salcantay, Pumasillo
	Cordillera Vilaconta	Ausangate
Tanzania	Kilimanjaro	Uhuru Peak
Turkey	Taurus Mountains	Ala Dag, Bolkar group
	Cilo Dag	Resko
	Agri Dag	Ararat
Uganda/Zaire	Ruwenzori	Stanley, Margeurite
USSR	Caucasus	Elbruz
	Pamirs	Pik Communisma, Pic Lenin
	Altai	Bieluka
	Chimbaluk	
Venezuela	Sierra Nevada de Merida	Pico Bolivar

CHOOSING AN OBJECTIVE

For your first expedition you would be well advised to attempt something not too ambitious. The ideal is a little-known cirque with a number of peaks to climb of varying difficulty. There are many such places scattered over the globe, although in this day and age you will be lucky indeed if you find somewhere that no one has been before. The danger of aiming at a difficult new route or a very high mountain is that you may find yourself susceptible to stomach trouble, you may discover that you do not acclimatize well, or you may be troubled more than you expected by being a long way from help. On a small expedition even one person suffering from one of these problems will influence what you can do and the way you do it. In addition, mountains never look anything like as big, steep or intimidating in photographs as they do when you are actually there. The reality can be something of a shock. And climbing in the greater ranges is just not the same as climbing in the Alps. Deep, unstable snow, enormous cornices and the sheer scale of things, as well as the altitude and remoteness – you will have to adjust to all these things.

There is a lot to be said for starting somewhere relatively close to home like northern Norway, Iceland, Spitzbergen or Turkey. The process of planning and or-

*Fig 8   Descending from Mount Kenya, a mountain over-equipped with
huts, including one on the summit, but a good place to experience
the effects of altitude and the need for acclimatization.*

ganization will teach you much, the travel in a foreign country will be fun and the mountaineering will be in a remote setting but without the seriousness or the expense of the greater ranges. In fact, such areas may well be quieter than many parts of Nepal, the Karakoram and Peru. For climbers in the United States, the Coast Range of British Columbia offers the same advantages, although if they are approached on foot some of their peaks are as difficult to reach as any in the world. Mount Kenya provides an excellent introduction to the problems of acclimatization and technical climbing at a fairly high altitude.

Do not be tempted to try a really big peak straight off. Reinhold Messner may be prone to melodrama, but he did not call the region above 8,000 metres 'the Death Zone' for nothing. Shortage of oxygen at altitude is not only the cause of pulmonary and cerebral oedema, but it can impair judgement and cause climbers to behave irrationally – leaving their gloves off, perhaps, or sitting bemused in a tent when they should be heading downwards. It also leads to total exhaustion; photos taken on the return from a high summit say it all, and many a fine climber has died by simply tripping over his crampons. High-altitude mountaineering is seductively glamorous from a distance, but it is desperately hard

Fig 9   *Bridges that have been swept away are a common cause of delay in the Himalaya.*

Fig 10   Roads are frequently washed away in the Himalaya, frustrating if you are short of time.

work and very dangerous. The ambition to reach the top of an 8,000-metre peak is understandable in a mountaineer, but only for a few do the rewards, spiritual or material, make it worthwhile more than once or twice; and many of them, sooner or later, do not come back. For most of us there is a wealth of more enjoyable climbing to be had at lower altitudes.

Time plays an important part in where you decide to go – not many people can afford the ten and a half months that Conway allowed himself for his expedition to the Karakoram in 1892. However, if you *do* have plenty of time, it is possible to live very cheaply in the East and to go on two or three expeditions for the price of one air

ticket. On the other hand, it is quite feasible to fit a lightweight expedition into the space of a three- or four-week annual holiday by visiting one of the countries mentioned above, or by going to South America or Alaska where access is easy and bureaucracy minimal. Do not visit the Himalaya if you are short of time, it will only lead to frustration: if the liaison officer is not a week late coming back from his wedding, the road will be blocked by a landslide or a Japanese expedition will have hired every porter in the vicinity. Time is worth far more than money. As Kipling put it:

'And the end of the fight is a tombstone white with the name of the late deceased,

And the epitaph drear "A fool lies here who tried to hustle the East".'

If you happen to be a lecturer, teacher or student with holidays that are generous but limited to July and August, you will have to forget about Nepal, Bhutan and much of the Indian Himalaya as the monsoon rains are at their heaviest in those months. In Alaska, too, the summer is statistically one of the worst times of year for weather, and crevasse bridges and cornices will be at their weakest. But you still have plenty of choice, including the Peruvian and Bolivian Andes where the southern winter is the dryest time of year. If you want a holiday over Christmas, there is Tierra del Fuego or Patagonia to consider, the volcanoes of Ecuador or Mexico further north, or Mount Kenya, Kilimanjaro and the Ruwenzori in Africa.

Cost is obviously an important factor. With luck, if you have climbed in the Alps you will already own most of the necessary equipment. The air fare (since it is probable that you will be travelling by air) is by far the biggest expense; everything else – food, accommodation, transport – will cost relatively little, wherever you go, as long as you are a small group travelling light. You can go on a lightweight climbing expedition almost anywhere in the world (including the Himalaya if you opt for a small peak), for less than £1,000 – well under, if you put your

Fig 11   A little-known cirque whose peaks are possibly still unclimbed . . .

Fig 12   A remote and probably unclimbed peak in Zanskar, a region of India which is far enough north not to be affected by the monsoon.

mind to it. Most Himalayan peaks, however, will cost twice that amount per climber, and in China or Bhutan the cost will be three or four times as much.

Finally, there is the question of what, if anything, you want out of your trip besides climbing. If contact with a different culture is appealing then the Himalaya or the Andes are the places to go. On the other hand, if you are attracted by the idea of big open spaces and wild animals, North America and the Arctic have more to offer. They are, of course, far from being mutually exclusive.

SOURCES OF INFORMATION

Deciding that you want to climb in big, remote, little-known mountains is one thing. Deciding exactly where to go is quite another. Even if you know that you want to visit, say, the Himalaya (despite the drawbacks), choosing an objective can still be a daunting task. The Himalaya is divided geographically into the Pamir, Hindu Kush, Karakoram, and Greater Himalaya, with infinite sub-divisions. Politically, it is divided between Afghanistan, Pakistan, Russia, China,

Nepal, India and Bhutan, and sub-divided into districts such as Swat, Zanskar, Kumaon, Manang, and so on. For the newcomer, it is bewildering and difficult to know where to begin.

The seed is usually sown by talking to friends and acquaintances, or going to a slide show that fires the imagination. This can be followed up by reading a book such as John Cleare's *Mountains and Mountaineering* (Collins 1979), which has fine photographs to whet the appetite and maps to put them into context, besides much useful information. Michael Kelsey's *Guide to the World's Mountains* (Cordee 1987) is helpful too. The next stage is to get more detailed information on the area which interests you – who has been there before, what peaks are still unclimbed, possible new lines, and so on. An exciting development is the Alpine Club's computerized Himalayan Index, designed to provide precisely that sort of information. However, it is still in its early stages and in the meantime there is no alternative to ploughing through back numbers of the *Alpine Journal*, the *American Alpine Journal* and the *Himalayan Journal*. As much interesting information is contained in the notes at the back of these journals as in the articles, but unfortunately only the *AAJ* includes them in its index.

As one would expect, the *HJ* has the most complete record of Himalayan climbing. The Himalaya Club newsletter is also a valuable resource if you want to keep right up to date with what has been happening. Although written in 1955, Kenneth Mason's *Abode of Snow* (Rupert Hart-Davis) still provides valuable background material, and has been reprinted recently by Diadem, while Louis Baume's *Sivalaya* (West Col 1978) is a bibliography for the 8,000-metre peaks.

For anything in North or South America

the *AAJ* is the best source of reference. Also useful for North America is the *Canadian Alpine Journal*, and invaluable for South America is Jill Neate's *Mountaineering in the Andes: a Source Book for Climbers*, published by the Expeditionary Advisory Centre. A topo guidebook now exists to the Cordillera Blanca and Cordillera Huyahuash (Philippe Beaud, Cordee 1988), but since it is written in three languages the information it can include is limited.

For the Arctic there is Mike Banks' *Greenland* (David and Charles 1975) and *Staunings Alps* (West Col 1972) by Donald Bennet, a guidebook to an area that was very popular in the late 1960s and early 1970s when the airstrip at Mestersvig was open. *Arctic Dreams* by Barry Lopez (Macmillan 1986) has nothing to do with mountaineering, but is a fascinating account of the history and ecology of the whole Arctic. *Mount McKinley Climber's Handbook* by Glen Randall (Genet Expeditions 1984) is useful for Alaskan climbing in general, although route information is confined to McKinley.

East Africa by Andrew Wielochowski (West Col 1986) is the most up-to-date guide for that part of the world covering Mount Kenya, Kilimanjaro and the Ruwenzori.

For other parts of the world, the *AJ*, the *AAJ* and *Mountain* magazine (also indexed) could all be useful, but do bear in mind that the activities of a multitude of small expeditions from non-English-speaking countries may not be recorded. This can lead to disappointment. To find a cairn, or, worse still, a tin can on your virgin summit is an anti-climax to put it mildly. On the other hand, to climb any peak in ignorance of its history is to enjoy all the excitement and uncertainty of a first ascent. As the number of climbers seeking new challenges overseas increases year by year, perhaps it is time to start researching our climbs less thoroughly and recording them less meticulously. Perhaps we should resist the temptation to leave proof that we have been to the summit, so that others can enjoy the same satisfaction. I like the story of the group from the North Island of New Zealand who, not so long ago, explored and climbed in a remote valley on South Island. Deliberately leaving behind maps and guidebooks, they had a wonderful (if strenuous) time discovering everything for themselves.

However, that is by the way. Journals, inevitably, are a year out of date by the time they appear. For more recent information, or more detail, you must quiz those who have just been there. In Britain, the BMC will often be able to supply names and addresses of expedition leaders. The Expedition Advisory Centre, run by the Young Explorers' Trust and the Royal Geographical Society, can do the same. In the United States, the American Alpine Club and the American Mountain Foundation both provide the same service for their members. The addresses of all these bodies and of useful reference libraries can be found in the Appendix.

Most climbers are happy to respond to enquiries; after all, they have been through the same fact-finding process themselves. However, you will receive the most help if you include a stamped-addressed envelope and make your questions as specific as possible. Do not expect an answer if you

Fig 13   The wide open spaces of Alaska – Mount Hess behind.

Fig 14   Ski-mountaineering in Kishtwar.

write 'Dear Sir, I plan to visit Nepal next year. I would be grateful for any information you can give me about climbing in this area.'!

Arguably the best source of information in Britain is one of the Alpine Climbing Group's sporadic social meets. The ACG came into existence in the 1950s, as a British counterpart to the Groupe d'Haute Montagne, an élite body of French alpinists. The idea of an élite never fitted comfortably into the British climbing scene but the ACG survived, thanks largely to the information contained in its *Bulletin*. This died a death some years ago, its function usurped by *Mountain* magazine and the *Alpine Journal*, but the ACG itself has moved with the times and

still exists. Its main rationale now is to provide a forum for disseminating information about the alpine-style activities of its members in the greater ranges. Its social evenings are open to all, and it would be strange if there was not someone there with first-hand knowledge of climbing almost anywhere in the world. Dates of ACG meets and the name and address of the Secretary can be obtained from the Alpine Club (*see* Appendix). Often these meets are arranged to coincide with an Alpine Club symposium on expedition mountaineering. Over the last few years these have been held annually at Plas y Brenin in North Wales and are an excellent way of gleaning information about specific areas.

As well as seeking information on your mountain, remember to find out as much as possible about the practical details of getting there. Ask questions like:

- What visas and vaccinations are necessary?
- How long does it take to get permission?
- How long do you need to spend in the capital city of the country concerned?
- Are there cheap but clean places to stay in the city?
- What is the best form of transport to the roadhead?
- What is the best form of transport from the roadhead to the mountain?
- Where can you buy mountain food and fuel?
- Where can you buy Base Camp and/or porters' food?
- What are the climbing seasons and weather patterns?

The Expedition Planners' Handbook and Directory, published annually by the Expedition Advisory Centre, is a mine of useful information, addresses and sources of reference. The EAC can also provide fact sheets on travel in different countries. Travellers' guides are now published to almost every corner of the world; Cordee are the distributors of an impressive number of titles. The BMC produces fact sheets for climbing in the Himalayan countries that are available on request.

MAPS

In Britain we have long been spoiled by the high quality of maps produced by the Ordnance Survey. We have only to go over the sea to Eire to realize that not all countries are so fortunate, though the Irish would maintain that it keeps alive the spirit of adventure ... Even well-surveyed maps in North America give no real indication of the steepness of the terrain. You can take nothing on trust: moderately close contours can mean anything from grass slopes to vertical cliffs, or from a snow plod to overhanging ice.

In Greenland, most maps are based on surveys made fifty years ago or more, and the occasional revision usually has not kept pace with glacial retreat. In the Himalaya, detailed maps at 1:50,000 exist, but are classified information only available on loan to a liaison officer. Various trekking maps are available, including a series covering the Indian Himalaya at 1:200,000 by Leomann Maps, distributed by West Col. It is possible to buy the US Army Map Service 1:250,000 sheets for most of the Himalaya, although these have only a limited use for trekking and none at all for climbing. In South America, the Austrian Alpine Club publishes Nevado Huascaran at 1:25,000, and Cordillera de Huayhuash and Cordillera Real at 1:50,000. West Col produce a map-guide series to Mount Ararat in Turkey, and to Mount Kenya, Kilimanjaro, the Ruwenzori and Mount Elgon in East Africa.

A visit to the Royal Geographical Society Map Room will give a good idea of what is available. Some, but not all, of their maps can be photocopied. To buy maps Stanfords International Map Centre in London is the place to go.

Most climbers will be better off than Felice Benuzzi and his friends whose only guide when they escaped from a prisoner-of-war camp to go climbing was a label from a bully-beef tin (*No Picnic on Mount Kenya*, William Kimber 1952). However, in many areas you will have to rely on sketch maps photocopied from journal articles. If these are to last the course, they need to be covered with 'transpaseal' or laminated.

PERMISSION

Expedition climbing in many parts of the world – McKinley, Logan, Fairweather, Baffin Island and Patagonia, for example – is within National Parks. Climbers are expected to register with the park authorities, but this usually can be done on the spot and there are few restrictions to which climbers can object. To climb in south and west Greenland permission must be sought from the Danish authorities but this is usually forthcoming within three months, provided you have proof of adequate insurance. Much of north and east Greenland lies within a single vast National Park. Permission to visit this area must be applied for by the end of the preceding year. At present, there are virtually no restrictions on climbing in the Andes; Aconcagua is the chief exception.

It is a different matter in the Himalayan countries – Pakistan, India, Bhutan, Nepal and Tibet (China). Permission must be applied for at least nine months in advance. More often than not, you will be told shortly before departure that the peak of your choice is not available and you must settle for second or third choice (although a recent trend on popular mountains has been to allow several expeditions to attempt the same route at the same time, creating potentially dangerous chaos). In China, it is usual for one expedition member to have to fly to Peking to sign the protocol beforehand.

It has been standard practice for many years to charge a hefty peak fee, varying with the height of the mountain, and to allocate to each expedition a liaison officer. From the point of view of the nations concerned, this system ensures that foreigners do not venture too close to politically-sensitive frontiers, it brings in useful foreign exchange, and it broadens the work experience of army and police officers. For the small expedition it doubles the size of the necessary budget. The officer's salary must be paid, and he must be equipped quite as well as the climbers, though the chances of his stepping beyond Base Camp are remote. To give him anything but the newest and best is asking for trouble, as its re-sale value at the end of the trip is what is important – much of his equipment will not be removed from its wrappers. The liaison officer will insist on having a cook to cater for him, and the cook will insist on a kitchen boy to help him. Probably a Sirdar will be regarded as necessary to organize the porters, and 'to keep in touch', a mail runner will be employed as well. All these people must be paid, clothed, fed and insured, and they do not carry loads. Sorting out this entourage and visiting the necessary government agencies is time-consuming, and usually means a week or more hanging around in Delhi, Kathmandu or Rawalpindi. For a large expedition, the whole procedure is sensible and the liaison officer's role as interpreter is undeniably useful, but for a small expedition the expense can be crippling and flexibility of movement is drastically curtailed.

If you are short of either time or money, it is sorely tempting to demonstrate the fundamental irresponsibility of climbing by doing so illegally. If you want to enjoy a mountain journey, climbing peaks along the way rather than operating from a Base Camp, you probably have no option but to

Fig 15   A liaison officer or a police escort is not a bad idea in some parts
of Pakistan where the local tribesmen are not at all friendly. In Peru, some
climbers have started to employ armed guards at base camps.

Fig 16   The author enjoying powder snow in Alaska. This sort of expedition is not easy in the Himalaya where liaison officers will not carry big packs and usually do not ski. However, if you are travelling rather than climbing peaks, an LO is not necessary.

do so. Provided you are content with little-known peaks and keep quiet about your achievements, this is actually quite feasible. The problem is that if you are indiscreet it could queer the pitch for everyone else. It also means that if you have an accident there is no back-up at all, and if you are forced to contact the authorities there will be big trouble. It behoves you to have your eyes wide open to the possible consequences of this approach. There are, after all, plenty of other places in the world where one can climb more freely and more cheaply.

Another way round the difficulty is to go as a large group to share the extra cost, and then split into smaller units to climb the mountain. Doug Scott has used this method a few times, establishing a Snell's Field type of base camp from which both climbers and families come and go. It sounds great fun, even though the element of isolation that can be so rewarding on a small, self-contained trip is lost.

Pakistan has recognized the needs of 'recreational climbers' by exempting all peaks under 6,000 metres from the usual rigmarole. This opens up boundless possibilities in the Hindu Kush, Hindu Raj and Karakoram. Nepal offers a number of so-called 'trekking peaks' (recently re-named 'Alpine Peaks') which give good climbing and are not to be underrated, but need only a Sirdar rather than a liaison officer.

Climbing in the USSR is restricted to carefully-regulated camps. In 1989 these are being held in the Caucasus, Pamirs, Altai and Chimbulak (this last including a winter camp for skiers).

A list of addresses to write to for permission can be found in the Appendix.

Most countries require a letter of endorsement from a national body before granting permission. In Britain, this role is filled by the British Mountaineering Council, in the US by the American Alpine Club. Their addresses are also in the Appendix.

A plentiful supply of 'mug-shots' of each climber is useful for dealings with bureaucracy. It also pays to remember that the bureaucrats who can make your life so difficult are human beneath their official exterior. A friendly manner and a cheerful smile are often all that are needed. Failing that, patience and courtesy may eventually win the day. Although it is easy to give way to bad temper and disrespect after hours or

31

Fig 17   A shepherd boy of the Karakoram with the sling-bow common in the region.

days of waiting, this will never have anything but a negative effect. A clean and tidy appearance helps too. Sometimes a little gift will work wonders. There is no such thing as a bribe ... it is merely a gift to show appreciation for services rendered – or about to be rendered – and should be offered with appropriate formality. Gifts that go down well in most countries are Scotch whisky (risky in Muslim countries, however), Swiss Army penknives and digital watches.

GRANTS

It is a sad but not unreasonable fact that if you want to climb in the greater ranges you are going to have to pay for most, if not all, of it yourself. Even the glamorous heavyweight trips to Everest and K2 have difficulty attracting sponsorship, and for a small expedition the chances of such blank-cheque treatment are virtually nil. The chances of obtaining gear free or at a reduced price are greater. Most firms are sympathetic and allocate part of their advertising or promotional budget specifically to helping expeditions; but their budgets are not unlimited and they prefer to help the big names, unless a project is definitely out of the ordinary. On the whole, it is wiser not to waste your money on headed notepaper or your time on begging letters. However, there are small grants worth applying for in both Britain and the US.

Britain

The main source of funds for small expeditions is the Mount Everest Foundation. This was set up with money raised after the 1953 expedition and topped up after the 1975

South-West Face expedition. Although it never underwrites an expedition, over the years its assistance has contributed enormously to the development of small-scale expeditionary mountaineering. At present its main criteria for making awards are experience and difficulty. If you have been on many expeditions and are attempting something hard, you will be given a relatively large grant (up to £1,300). If you are less experienced and have a modest objective, your grant will be a token gesture. In some ways this is fair enough, yet it is the younger and less experienced climbers who are often the most impecunious and in need of help. Most parties which receive an MEF grant will also be eligible for a similar grant from the British Mountaineering Council (government-funded by the Sports Council).

Other grants available are: the Nick Estcourt Award, specifically for a lightweight expedition; the Alison Chadwick Fund for women; and the Mick Burke Award for expedition film-making. In Scotland, the Sang Award is administered by the Scottish Mountaineering Club.

Names and addresses to write to are in the Appendix.

USA

The American Alpine Club has a Mountaineering Fellowship Fund from which a limited number of grants of $300–750 are made every year to climbers under the age of twenty-six.

The AAC also administers the Vera Watson/Alison Chadwick Memorial Fund which gives grants to 'Individuals, both male and female, who are participating in expeditions with a significant mountaineering objective for women'.

Approved expeditions and individuals can receive loans from the AAC. These are interest-free for six months but must be paid back within a year.

Both the AAC and the American Mountaineering Foundation run sponsorship programmes in which donations made to approved expeditions are tax-deductible.

INSURANCE

Insurance is an expensive extra and, one hopes, never needed, but it is *essential*. Whether you wish to insure your personal belongings is up to you, but the cost of rescue and evacuation from remote areas and of medical treatment overseas is so astronomic that it would be plain foolishness to consider going on an expedition without cover. Moreover, bitter experience has caused the authorities in some areas to adopt a hard line. Joe Simpson lay untreated in hospital in Peru for two days until authorization was received from his insurance company (*Touching the Void*, Jonathan Cape 1988).

Some insurance brokers will quote a premium based on an assessment of the team's experience and the nature of its objective. Others will simply add a 50 per cent loading for mountaineering on to a standard expedition package. For reasons not wholly logical, ski-mountaineering involves an additional loading. At the time of writing it is worth allowing at least £80 a head ($100) to insure for a two-month trip. Be sure to read the small print carefully so you are clear about what you are entitled to claim for.

Many insurance companies will not handle expeditions. Addresses of some that do are given in the Appendix.

Some countries demand a bond to be left with them to pay for helicopter rescue. It is returned at the end of the expedition but needs to be budgeted for. In Bhutan it is US $3,000, and in Pakistan US$4,000. The Danish (Greenland) and Nepalese authorities insist on seeing proof of insurance or a bank guarantee before they will permit an expedition to go ahead and visit their countries.

MEDICINE

An expedition, especially in the East, can be a pill-taker's paradise. There are pills for malaria, pills for purifying water, antibiotics for preventing stomach infection, and, because they often cause diarrhoea, more pills to cope with that; then there are vitamin and iron tablets, sleeping tablets and pills to prevent mountain sickness and frostbite; finally, it is not unknown for climbers to carry amphetamines, ostensibly for an emergency. I have not the slightest doubt that there are climbers who routinely take every one of these pills and a few more besides. Most, however, certainly are not necessary.

So, what *should* you take? Well, even purists would be advised to take pills for malaria and water purification (more of that later). If you know that you have a weak stomach or acclimatize very slowly, then there may be a case for taking drugs prophylactically. Otherwise it seems more sensible to give your body a chance to adapt and save drugs for when they are really needed. If they are going over 3,500 metres women should avoid the contraceptive pill, because it makes the body more liable to retain fluid and the blood is therefore more likely to clot.

*Fig 18   Often the medical kit is scarcely used, but in the event of an
accident much of it will be needed. Here, the climbers are not
wearing helmets, unwise on this sort of terrain.*

Fig 19   This climber was suffering from bad blisters through wearing heavy boots on the walk-in. In this sort of environment any wound takes a long time to heal and easily goes septic.

My personal first aid kit on a mountain consists of:

ITEM	FOR
Panadol	Headaches
Fortral or Pethidine	Severe pain
Imodium	Diarrhoea
Melolin	(Non-adhesive dressing) large wounds or blisters
Zinc oxide tape	Non-medical repairs and strapping for wounds
Elastoplast dressing	Small cuts and blisters
Crepe bandage	General-purpose bandaging as well as support for sprains

However, a much more comprehensive medical kit is necessary at Base Camp: dysentery is no fun and an accident will be very serious. You will probably need to consult your doctor about inoculations and he or she will usually be happy to advise about a medical kit and even put it together for you. A doctor or nurse in the party makes life simple and is a great reassurance, although all doctors seem to feel naked without a far larger and heavier medical kit than you or I might carry! If you are not fortunate enough to have a doctor or nurse, everybody in the party should at least have attended a first-aid course recently, preferably one related to mountaineering. This is a good idea, anyway, as doctors are not immune to disease and injury. Good courses are run at Plas y Brenin, National Centre for Mountain Activities, in North Wales and by WEST (addresses in the Appendix). *Medicine for Mountaineering* by James A. Wilkerson (The Mountaineers of Seattle, 1985) goes well beyond first aid. It could be a useful book to have with you if things go wrong, and also provides hours of interesting reading if they don't. The Mountain Medicine Data Centre, St Bartholomew's Hospital, London is run on a voluntary basis by Dr Charles Clarke and can provide fact sheets at £2 on many aspects of mountaineering medicine.

For a discussion of medical problems likely to be encountered *see* sections on food and drink on the walk-in (Chapter 3) and medical problems (Chapter 5).

The following is a suggested medical kit for a three-person expedition of four to six weeks, operating from a base camp:

4 boxes Elastoplast adhesive dressing strip
30 Melolin non-adhesive dressings (10 x 10cm)
3 rolls zinc oxide tape
1 roll tubular dressing for fingers
1 large roll cotton wool
1 large roll gauze
3 sterile wound dressings
3 crepe bandages (3in)
2 triangular bandages
2 pkts steristrip wound closures
1 scalpel blade
3 sterilized needles
12 safety pins
1 pair scissors
1 full-leg inflatable splint
1 bottle antiseptic liquid
1 tube zinc and castor oil cream
1 tube Betnovate for skin allergy, bad sunburn
1 tube Chloromycetin ointment for eye infections
1 ampoule Amethocaine drops for snow blindness
Cough sweets
Insect repellent
Flea powder
1 Tineafax foot powder
1 pack Anusol suppositories for piles
20 Piriton – anti-histamine for stings and allergic reactions
20 Aludrox for indigestion
20 Dulcolax for constipation
300 Imodium for diarrhoea
30 Maxolon – anti-spasmodic
20 Euhypnos – sleeping pill
200 Panadol for mild pain
50 Fortral for severe pain
20 Pethidine for very severe pain
3 courses Septrin or other broad-spectrum antibiotic
3 courses Flagyl for amoebic dysentery or giardiasis
3 courses Furamide – follow-up to Flagyl
10 Decadron (dexamethasone) for pulmonary or cerebral oedema

Fig 20   Girl in a Himalayan village. People are often badly in need of medical help but unwilling or unable to travel to a hospital.

More often than not very little of this kit will be used and it will seem like so much unnecessary weight. However, if there is one serious wound or a fracture in your party, much of it will be needed.

In third-world countries climbers face a dilemma. As they walk through the country-side they are frequently confronted by appalling illness and disease and asked for help. Even for doctors it is a problem as they are only passing through and their supply of drugs is not infinite. For the layman it is probably better not to intervene at all unless it is a matter of cleaning an obviously dirty wound. A good supply of extra Panadol and plasters can help with minor complaints, but beware of hypochondriacs and pill hoarders.

HAUTE CUISINE

Nutrition is a complicated subject but it seems that a balanced diet is made up of roughly 50 per cent carbohydrate, 30 per cent fat and 20 per cent protein. Fats are the most efficient form of food in terms of calories for weight, and for that reason polar rations have always been based on fatty meats like pemmican, and butter. Protein is essential for the building and repair of cells, although the average western diet contains far more than necessary. Unfortunately, the breaking down of protein uses up quantities of fluid and this can contribute to dehydration, while both proteins and fats require more oxygen to be converted into energy than carbohydrates. It makes sense at altitude, therefore, to have a diet based on carbohydrates, say 70 per cent, with the remaining 30 per cent provided by fats and proteins. If you are climbing at relatively low altitudes, below 5,000 metres, you can afford to reduce the weight of your rations by having a higher proportion of fats. As long as the diet is reasonably varied, most of the minerals and vitamins required by the body will be present automatically, and most mountaineering expeditions, especially lightweight ones, are not in the hills long enough for deficiencies to become a problem. Carolyn Gunn discusses the whole topic in detail in *The Expedition Cookbook* (Chockstone Press).

Everybody has their own ideas about food and they differ widely, from the legendary sack of tsampa favoured by Shipton and Tilman to the freeze-dried boeuf stroganoff and strawberries and cream preferred by expeditions with money to spend. In fact, tsampa is an excellent food, although it is usually only available in the drier Tibetan parts of the Himalayas. It is made from barley which is roasted before being ground, and the resultant flour can be mixed with water, tea, vegetables or even eaten dry. It is cheap, filling and needs no cooking. What more do you want? To our pampered palates tsampa may be bland, but it is well worth buying a sack of it and experimenting.

By contrast to tsampa, freeze-dried food is extremely expensive and not even as light as people claim when you consider the weight of the packaging and the unrealistic size of the portions offered. The freeze-dried myth was effectively exploded by Ron Gregg in an article in *Mountain 79* entitled 'Food for Thought'. In addition, however much one may feel that 'meat and two veg' are essential for a healthy diet, both lose their appeal at altitude and, speaking for myself, biscuits and jam, and muesli become much more attractive. Doug Scott prefers to carry a bag of lentils or beans pre-cooked at base camp. Freeze-dried foods can have a part to play, especially lower down, but given the prohibitive cost of excess baggage

Fig 21   Haute cuisine – chapattis for breakfast.

and the hassles involved with air freight, it is best to buy the bulk of your food locally and in most third-world countries this will preclude freeze-dried items. In the cities of Asia and South America and in the settlements of the Arctic it is possible to buy a limited range of dried foods, and in Kathmandu there is a thriving market not just in gear but in surplus expedition rations. Exactly what you take on the hill will be determined by where you are and what you can buy. Suffice it to say that sensitive taste-buds are a distinct disadvantage on an expedition; the ability to shovel down food because it is fuel that you need is invaluable.

If you can fit some food into your pack on the journey out, tea-bags, milk powder and instant soups are among the most useful items, followed by potato powder, fruit drinks and stews. A range of drinks makes it easier to get down enough fluid to prevent dehydration, and drinks that are full of calories (like sweet tea and cocoa) kill two birds with one stone.

Allowing for packaging the ration opposite gives about 900g or 2lb per person per day. I have never checked the calorific content but it seems to work, although you do not put on weight.

It is worth having a plentiful supply of your own polythene bags (including bin-liners) and containers, so that you can re-pack food, reducing its weight and bulk. In the third world poly bags are not easily come by and plastic bottles usually leak. For transporting food to the mountain sacks are readily available, as are large used biscuit tins for breakable or squashable items.

Typical no-frills ration used on several small expeditions.

ITEM	GRAMS PER PERSON PER DAY
Tea (six bags)	15
Coffee	5
Cocoa	25
Sugar	90
Milk	30
Fruit crystals	15
Soup	25
Dehydrated stew	75
Potato or pasta	30
Dried vegetables	15
Muesli	75
Plain biscuits	90
Margarine	20
Cheese	30
Jam	20
Chocolate	120
Dried fruit	60
	740 grams

Fig 22 Sacks and old biscuit tins are easily procured for transporting food, but they need to be lined with plastic bags. Moving your kit from A to B sometimes calls for improvisation.

Alternatives are to have a tailor make up some canvas kit-bags, or buy metal trunks (which have the advantage that they can be locked) in the bazaar. However you travel, the food has a long way to go, it is going to be roughly handled, and it will quite probably get wet at some stage. You need to pack accordingly.

THE PARTY

On a small expedition it would seem obvious that you will be going with your friends. But it is worth considering *which* of your friends. Someone who is good company in the pub may not be so congenial after three days storm-bound in a tent. Anyone who has a volatile temper or an aggressive manner, or who is subject to fits of depression is bad news on an expedition,

41

however gifted they may be technically. The smaller the party, the more trying they will be to live with. The real success of the trip is going to depend not on whether you reached the summit, but whether you come home feeling you did your best and are still friends with your companions. Some expeditions, apparently successful and given a big splash in the magazines, have been total disasters in human terms. Sometimes honourable failure may be more satisfying than divisive success. In this goal-obsessed age, it is worth remembering the wise words of H. W. Tilman:

'A man ought to rate his achievements only by the satisfaction they give him, for they will soon be outdone, outshone and speedily forgotten by everyone but himself.'

It is pointless to deny that there will be tensions and conflict at times on any expedition, as there are in any relationship; but at the end of the day, a successful expedition enhances friendships rather than destroys them. And if the peak is climbed as well, so much the better. In fact, the two tend to go hand in hand. A harmonious team is more likely to be determined, well-organized and able to put all its weight behind a 'push' than one riven by bickering and ill-feeling. So give some thought to whom you go with, and make sure you all get away for a few weekends together, preferably camping in bad weather. It sounds obvious, but it is surprising how often it doesn't happen.

How many should be in the party? Solo climbs in glaciated terrain are always hazardous; even a rope of two runs a risk of disappearing for ever down a crevasse, and has the added disadvantage that if one person falls sick the other is stuck. Four

seems a logical number – safer, more companionable, and able to operate as two ropes of two – yet there is the distinct danger of an 'us and them' mentality developing when you cook and sleep in separate tents. Chris Bonington became conscious of this even with such seasoned companions as Boardman, Tasker and Renshaw, when they were cooking as two pairs in a snow cave on the North-East Ridge of Everest (*Everest: the Unclimbed Ridge*, W. W. Norton 1983). Even if this polarization into pairs does not occur, there is a greater chance of one person feeling left out or isolated in a four than in a three. Some modern research suggests that the old adage should be modified to 'three's company, four's a crowd'.

If three people share a tent, they use almost exactly the same camping and climbing gear as a pair, but the weight can be split three ways – a distinct advantage. With good rope management, three are only slightly slower than two. The lead climber can bring up the other two at the same time using a double sticht plate, for instance; alternatively, the second belays the leader while number three jumars or prusiks. If you are using only one rope to save weight, the second and third climbers simply tie on ten feet apart and climb together; by tying in with a long loop, the second can reduce the chance of one off meaning both off (Fig 23). On corniced ridges as well as on glaciers, the third person and the extra rope out is a safety factor. All in all, three seems to be the ideal number for a lightweight expedition.

One member of the party must assume the role of leader. Once on the mountain it becomes irrelevant, but for the purpose of applying for grants and permission and dealing with officialdom it is necessary.

Fig 23   A long tie-in loop for the middle person of a rope of three. Some advocate a second knot, overhand or figure of eight, a few inches from the karabiner to prevent slack sliding through it, which might cause shock loading.

TRAINING

Personal preparation for an expedition has varied wildly between individuals, and still does. Eric Shipton took to carrying pig-nuts borrowed from a local farmer up Clee Hill in Shropshire. Don Whillans believed that you lost so much weight on the mountain that it was a wise precaution to put on plenty beforehand, and drinking beer was the most efficient way of doing it. Alex MacIntyre, with an equal liking for beer, argued that a hangover was the only realistic way of simulating the effects of altitude. Reinhold Messner has always been more thorough. In his first book, *The Seventh Grade* (Kaye and Ward 1974), he describes how he trained for Nanga Parbat:

'I had worked out that every kilogram of surplus weight in climbing uses up calories and therefore oxygen. I also realised that the legs have the hardest job to do, so I began to develop my thighs and calves rather than the muscles of my torso. I therefore stopped climbing and went in for uphill running. I did a daily uphill run from Bolzano to

Jenesien. I did this 1,000 metres on my toes without a rest and it took me less than an hour. At the same time, I did breathing exercises and ate and drank at extended intervals in order to accustom my kidneys to extreme conditions.

'Normally I eat little meat, mainly carbohydrates and a lot of fruit. In order to be sure of a bowel movement, I instituted a day of fruit once a week and drank a lot of milk. I ate a lot of garlic before I set off for Nanga Parbat as I had read that it increased the elasticity of the vascular walls ... After a few months I really began to enjoy my training and I often did long periods of running. My morning cold showers had become a habit and even now I cannot do without them.'

Messner, it has to be recognized, has climbed all fourteen 8,000-metre peaks and is still alive. It's worth listening to his opinions. For those who are less ambitious than Messner, but still keen to succeed in their objective, the uphill running seems a good idea, but perhaps the cold showers and the garlic need not be taken too seriously.

2   Equipment

On my first expedition to the big mountains I had single leather boots, woollen breeches and no overtrousers. We made ourselves overboots out of deckchair canvas (very colourful but no use whatever), we used ex-WD pack-frames that were hideously uncomfortable but could be piled high with boxes, tents and kit-bags, and we slept on bulky foam mattresses that quickly mopped up condensation from the groundsheet. Looking back, it all sounds ludicrously inadequate. Yet we had a wonderful time, journeying up wild valleys, crossing cols, exploring glaciers and climbing new peaks, and we returned home thinner and wiser than when we started.

I mention this only because there is so much gear on the market now, and so much being spent on persuading us to buy it, that it is easy to lose sight of what we really need. Most of this gear is extremely functional and often stylish too (sometimes it's the other way round . . .), but if you are faced with the choice of buying the necessary gear and going climbing, go climbing. The gear will look after itself. If you have enough to

Fig 24   Comparing notes on the overland drive through Afghanistan.

Fig 25   Equipment has come a long way in the last twenty years.

climb in the Alps, you can climb pretty well anywhere under 6,500 metres, except perhaps Mount McKinley. Unless you really want to push back the frontiers of the possible, don't feel you must buy new clothing and equipment to go on an expedition. I prefer to use old gear anyway, partly because I know it is going to get hammered and partly because I know it works or is comfortable. If your sleeping bag keeps you warm, your waterproofs keep you almost dry, and your tent stays upright over a wild, wet November weekend in the Llanberis Pass, you are equipped well enough for most things.

PERSONAL EQUIPMENT

A good sleeping bag is the first essential, preferably filled with down for its lightness and small volume when compressed. Bulk is always going to be as much of a problem as weight. Struggling to squeeze a mountain of gear, not to mention food and fuel, into a rucksack that seems enormous when you buy it but is never, in fact, quite large enough, seems to be an inescapable part of mountaineering. With down, weight equals warmth equals price – the more down you have the warmer the bag will be and the more it will cost. The only real variable is that goose-down is fluffier than duck-down and so traps more air, which is what makes down or any other insulation warm in the first place.

There are various different constructions but basically the manufacturers ensure that their quality bags (those filled with down as opposed to feathers or a feather-down mix) will have the most effective construction. For most purposes a bag with 900 grams of

goose-down should see you right. On an 8,000-metre peak you might want to opt for 1,100 grams or more, if you can afford it. A zip down one side is handy for ventilating the bag in warm weather, but it weighs more, costs more and is always a potential weakness. Down bags are not cheap but they do last a long time. I have one which was the inner of a double bag issued by the British Antarctic Survey in 1970. After I had lived in it for a year nobody was interested in taking it back, so I brought it home. With some difficulty I found a dry-cleaner prepared to touch it, and I have been using it ever since! It has served me well on twenty-odd expeditions and countless camps and bivouacs in Britain and the Alps. I have washed it once or twice and if the loft is not quite what it used to be, it still keeps me warm most of the time.

If a good sleeping bag is essential, insulation from beneath is equally important, and come by far more cheaply. A 'five seasons karrimat' (or two thinner ones) will do the trick, but it is a bulky item. The best way to carry it is rolled up on the side of your pack, secured by the compression straps; a couple of extra straps are handy to keep it rolled up when packing. A 'thermarest' – an insulated mat that is also inflatable – is a popular alternative. It is more comfortable than a karrimat, but also heavier, more expensive and liable to puncture. That said, those who own them swear by them. Ideally, your combined mats should cover the floor area of the tent; it is a false economy to skimp on size or length when you are camping on snow.

A gore-tex bivi-bag is useful not just for bivis but also to protect your sleeping bag in a tent or snow cave from water vapour produced by cooking, and from hoar frost that builds up on the tent walls, not to

Fig 26   The morning after the night before.

mention loose snow, spilled tea and globs of porridge. At cold temperatures, gore-tex does not work perfectly: the microscopic pores of the gore-tex membrane become choked with ice so that water vapour from the body condenses on the inside of the bag instead of passing through it. Over a period of days, the sleeping bag will become damp and it is a good idea to air it whenever the chance arises. Nevertheless, a bivi-bag definitely keeps the sleeping bag drier than it would be without, increases its overall warmth by creating an extra layer of warm air, and enables one to sleep outside if need be. An alternative is a sleeping bag made of gore-tex. This is a lighter and less bulky combination, but not so warm and, lacking the large closeable hood of a bivi-bag, it

does not afford the same protection on a bivouac. Such bags cannot be bought on the open market. The material has to be bought directly from Gore Ltd and then made up specially by a manufacturer.

At very cold temperatures a proofed-nylon inner bag will act as a vapour barrier. Water vapour from the body cannot pass through it to damp the down or form as hoar frost on the bivi-bag, yet because it is inside the sleeping bag there is a very small temperature gradient and so very little condensation. The body is cocooned in warm air, no heat is lost through evaporation and the sleeping bag remains dry. The only snag is that in less than extreme conditions a vapour barrier is too hot and becomes unpleasantly sticky. To avoid the

47

extra weight of an inner bag and the uncomfortable twisting and constricting it can cause as you turn over at night, it is possible to have the inside of a sleeping bag made of an impermeable material. This system was used successfully on the 'Foot-steps of Scott' expedition in the Antarctic, but it is a highly specialised piece of kit. It is probably more versatile to have a separate vapour barrier bag which need not be used until high on the mountain. At lower altitudes it can be used to up-grade an old sleeping bag.

A vapour barrier is also effective on the feet, worn as a nylon sock which prevents the normal sock and the inner boot from becoming damp. Another thin sock is worn next to the skin for comfort and this needs to be dried off at night. The tendency is for feet, socks and inner boots to become soaking wet inside plastic boots, anyway, so the vapour barrier is enhancing their in-sulating properties by keeping them dry and reducing the amount of drying out necessary at night. Some inner boots are made of Alveolite, a closed-cell foam which is very warm, very light, and does not absorb moisture; in fact, it is a vapour barrier in its own right, making a vapour barrier sock redundant. Some people carry powder to help dry and air their feet. Whether or not you use a vapour barrier, it is important to carry a spare pair of socks to change into at night while the other pair is drying inside your clothes or sleeping bag.

Yeti gaiters (or 'super-gaiters') are useful for keeping snow out of your boots and adding a little extra insulation. On very high or very cold climbs, where any rock will be climbed in crampons, an overboot is worth-while, insulating the sole of the foot as well as the upper.

As for clothing, most people take too much rather than too little, and regret it when they have to start carrying it. In general, the equipment you would use on a serious route in the Alps will suffice on peaks of a similar altitude in most parts of the world, and up to 6,500 metres in the Andes and Himalayas. Bear in mind, though, that April and October will be considerably colder than July wherever you are.

Many garments are now made with a zip from navel to back, or a zipped 'crap-flap' to enable you to perform bodily functions without taking off any clothes. It is obviously important that *all* your lower garments are equipped with this facility. Care is needed when using it; some very unfortunate incidents have occurred . . . Personally, I have always found it quite possible to drop my trousers in even the wildest weather and, if not exactly pleasant, the chances of disaster are considerably less. This simple solution to the problem does, however, depend on wearing trousers rather than salopettes or braces.

A down jacket and down boots (with waterproof bottoms for short trips out into the snow) are pleasant luxuries to have in any snow camping situation, but they *are* luxuries on 6,000-metre peaks in summer conditions. They become more important the higher you go, and the earlier or later in the year you are climbing. Down trousers and one-piece suits are specialist items only necessary on 8,000-metre peaks, or major winter ascents.

A good rucksack is obviously important. On most trips, heavy, bulky loads have to be carried at some stage, and the best pack for the job, with an internal frame and a capacity of at least 90 litres, will weigh about 2.5kg. On the actual climb, you want to be carrying as little extra weight as possible. Alex MacIntyre reckoned that it ought to be possible to make a 75-litre rucksack out of lightweight materials weighing 1kg or less. The saving in weight would be equivalent to two days' food. He persuaded Karrimor to make just such a sack and it has been used successfully on many expeditions since. However, it is not comfortable with a load of over 20kg. The ideal is two sacks, a heavy one for load-carrying, a light one for climbing. On the approach, the big pack can be carried by a porter or used as a container. However, if you are undertaking a long ski journey or unsupported trek through the mountains, you will be better off with a single large-volume, heavy-duty pack, despite the weight.

Fig 27 Here the climbers have only small rucksacks so need a pack-frame to carry tents and boxes of food. Nowadays, climbers use large-volume rucksacks, usually with an internal frame, and would have dispensed with the cardboard boxes by this stage.

49

Fig 28   The lightweight, no-frills 'Macsac' on the left, and a giant 120-litre Condor pack on the right.

Check-list of personal equipment for a 6,500-metre peak in the Karakoram during July and August:

Down sleeping bag
Gore-tex bivi-bag
Five seasons karrimat
Tent boots
Vest, shirt, sweater
Pile jacket
Pile trousers or salopettes
Gore-tex jacket
Gore-tex overtrousers
Wool or pile mitts with windproof outers
Spare mitts, also with windproof outers
Finger gloves
Wool hat or headband
Balaclava
Sun hat or peaked cap
Plastic boots with standard inners
Yeti gaiters
2 pairs socks
75-litre rucksack
Helmet
Harness
Prusik loops
Sun screen, lip salve
Sunglasses
Goggles
Headtorch and Duracell battery
Water bottle
Mug, spoon
Penknife

Compass and Altimeter

A compass can be handy wherever you are, if only for a general idea of direction. Russell Brice and Harry Taylor would have been glad of one at the top of the North East Ridge of Everest ... Climbers from Europe need to remember that the magnetic variation in North America is far from negligible as it is in the Alps – it is about 27° east in the Alaska Range – and that they will have to subtract it when they would normally add it and vice versa. In the southern hemisphere a compass adjusted to cater for the dip of the needle makes life a lot easier.

An altimeter can be used in three ways: as a barometer; to tell you how far you have climbed at a stretch; and as an aid to navigation in poor visibility. The last is its most useful function but only when used with accurate maps marked with a number of spot heights. These are needed so that the reading can be recalibrated frequently to allow for fluctuations in pressure. Generally, maps are not going to be so detailed so do not rush out to buy one specially.

Cameras

It is a rare climber who does not own and use a camera. I sometimes have misgivings about our obsession with photography – I wonder if it is not really a form of acquisitiveness, a desire to preserve and hoard experience which can lead, if we are not careful, to postponing the experience until the slides come back. The ecstatic moment is all too easily lost in a welter of technical considerations about lighting, shutter speeds or depth of field, and a preoccupation with composing the scene into an acceptable rectangle. It is sad to

reach a summit and to think chiefly in terms of how it will look through the viewfinder. On occasions I have found myself positively grateful that I have run out of film or my camera has broken, leaving me free to climb or ski or walk purely for the sake of the activity and not for the recording of it.

Yet there are equally times when it is satisfying to try to use a camera creatively: to capture the drama of a climb, or the peacefulness of an evening when the action is over, to seek the essence of sky or water or rock, or to convey the meaning of wilderness. Even if we fail, the effort is worthwhile if it makes us respond more perceptively to our surroundings. And our memories are sadly fallible when it comes to remembering details of treasured experiences.

Perhaps the answer is to be consciously selective, to photograph memorable moments or visually striking scenes, but not to feel obliged to take home a blow by blow record of the trip. As well as leaving one freer to live for the present rather than for the future, it will reduce the amount you spend on film.

Cameras can be heavy and cumbersome. Although it is fun to show friends and family slides of your deeds of derring-do, unless you take photographs for a living or know that you can make money out of lecturing, it may be better to concentrate on the mountaineering and forget about reflex cameras and interchangeable lenses. There are several sophisticated miniature cameras with excellent lenses on the market, which will fit into a shirt pocket and are ideal for climbing. Only slightly more bulky are a host of fairly cheap automatic cameras that take very passable pictures. Some of these respond to the brightness of snow by underexposing the scene as a whole. It becomes necessary to fool the exposure meter by adjusting the film speed setting to compensate – for example, adjusting a setting of 64ASA to 125 or even 200. It is worth experimenting beforehand.

These little cameras usually have a fairly wide angle lens with a focal length of 30mm to 40mm. Basically, this means that you see a lot in the viewfinder but pay for it with slight distortion: objects near the lens appear disproportionately large, objects in the distance become smaller. This means that in a landscape, the mountains shrink a little and it is important to fill the foreground with something interesting. The best climbing shots are usually taken when the subject is only a few feet away; half a rope length reduces a climber to a distant speck of colour. Once these constraints are recognized, it is possible to take excellent pictures with a miniature camera. It is the photographer who counts, not the equipment.

If you do decide to take a single-lens reflex, you can reduce the weight and still cover most situations by using a 35–105mm macro zoom. The macro facility is useful for photographing flowers; the 105mm end of the lens is good for portraits or pulling the mountains in close. A useful extra if you are taking photography seriously is a clamp for attaching the camera to an ice-axe; this will enable you to take time-exposures of moonlit mountain-scapes or of dawn breaking.

Whatever sort of camera you use, a UV (ultraviolet) filter is well worth having. It prevents blue shadows appearing in snow scenes and blue skies from turning black, and also protects the lens from scratches and dirt.

Dust is a problem in hot countries, so keeping your camera in a poly bag as well as a case is a good idea. The camera bags made of closed-cell foam that are widely available (Lowe-Pro, Camera Care and Karrimor all produce a range) are very effective at keeping out dust, rain or snow and protecting the camera against knocks. Above the snow line, avoid taking a camera out of its case in a warm tent, as condensation will form as soon as you take it outside again. This means that lens and filter must be cleaned before you can use the camera, and may cause moving parts to freeze up. It is normally safer to leave the camera outside in a rucksack. However, in very cold temperatures shutters are liable to freeze and batteries to fail. The only solution is to keep the camera with you, inside your sleeping bag at night and inside your clothing by day.

When you rewind a film into its cassette, it is worth leaving the leader protruding, as bright light can sometimes leak into the film. If you do this it is easy to forget whether or not that film has been used, so, rather than risk double-exposing, partially tear the end of the leader.

Nowadays, most airports use X-ray machines that do not damage film, but just in case it is worth keeping all film with you in your hand baggage and producing it at the security check.

Whether to take prints or slides is a matter of choice. Prints are easier to look at or show friends, but colour print quality is often disappointing, and for any sort of publication, slides will be preferred. If you opt for prints, consider taking black and white rather than colour – they will be cheaper to blow up and will be just as expressive. One has only to glance through Fosco Maraini's books *Karakoram* (Hutchinson 1961) and *Where Four Worlds Meet* (Hamish Hamilton 1964), not to mention Ponting's *Great White South* (Duckworth

1921), to realize that colour does not have the last word in expedition photography. My own favourite mountain picture, of two exuberant tribesmen on a windswept pass in the Hindu Kush, is in Wilfred Thesiger's collection of superb black and white photographs, *Desert, Marsh and Mountain* (Collins 1979).

Personal Stereos

Personal stereo cassette players have come to be seen almost as a necessity on climbing expeditions. However, they have definite disadvantages that are worth considering before you decide to take one.

When tapes and spare batteries are included they are both bulky and heavy. If you want to be self-contained and mobile rather than operating from a fixed camp, this is a factor to concern you.

Music provides escape or insulation from the listener's surroundings. This may seem an advantage during frustrating delays when a road is blocked or the porters are on strike, yet why travel in a foreign country if you immediately seek the security of your own culture?

At Base Camp or on the mountain stereos can isolate people from each other and cause a team to fragment just when companionship and support may be most needed. There is nothing more demoralizing than lying in a tent next to someone who is wired-in, with their eyes shut, when you feel the need to talk. Reading a book never creates quite the same sense of inaccessibility.

Retreat from a boring or frightening reality may be tempting, but listening to familiar tunes with all their associations with home and loved-ones can accentuate homesickness and weaken resolve, with serious consequences.

Finally, music, like hot baths and fresh bread, is one of those luxuries that we can very well do without, but which we appreciate all the more when we return to civilization. The ascetic ideal is not a fashionable one; yet the more creature comforts we insist on taking with us, the less we are likely to derive from a sojourn in the hills. The expedition becomes more a gladiatorial struggle with a mountain than a contact with wilderness, which seems a pity.

TENTS

Modern mountain tents tend to be domes or tunnels, or hybrids nicknamed 'dunnels' or 'geo-hybrids', which incorporate the geodesic design of the one with the rectangular floor shape of the other. The theory behind geodesic tents is that they are made up of a series of angled panels that spill the wind, rather than a single large surface that must give before it. They are roomier inside than traditional A-frame tents, and they are free-standing so that anchors are purely to hold them down rather than give them their shape. The other side of the coin is that an A-frame tent is half the price of a dome, need weigh no more, and is quicker and easier to pitch. It is also easier to repair the poles. Technology has moved on, but it is still an effective design that has served mountaineers well in the past. Let no one be deterred from going into the big hills because they cannot afford the latest and most costly of geodesic designs.

In any tent, an entrance at each end is a great asset: two people can leave or enter at the same time, or one end can be used for cooking, with the other as an entrance. A valance round the outside adds slightly to the weight, and the lumps of ice that sometimes stick to it overnight can be troublesome, but on balance the extra security afforded makes it worthwhile. It prevents the wind lifting up the flysheet, and blocks of snow, food and gear can be piled on it to help hold the tent down in a big blow. Some tents have poles threaded through the flysheet and the tent suspended from them. This means that tent and fly can be carried and pitched as a single unit, saving time and eliminating the possibility of the fly blowing away.

One problem encountered with modern tents is that the shock-cord linking the poles can lose its elasticity at very low temper-atures. This is infuriating and can easily lead to frostbitten fingers in bad conditions. There is no easy solution, although it helps to keep the poles well insulated inside your pack during the day, and to put them together immediately on stopping to camp.

In the Arctic and Antarctic where, in the summer, it is often preferable to travel at night, a pale-coloured flysheet combined with a dark inner make the tent both cooler and more restful for sleeping during the heat and brightness of the day.

Some tents are made of a single skin of gore-tex to save weight. I am suspicious of these, having spent some uncomfortable days and nights at a wet Base Camp trying

Fig 29   The strongest tent in the world? Unfortunately these two-person pyramid tents used in Antarctica weigh 70lb!

*Fig 30 An old-fashioned mountain tent – very heavy and totally dependent
on the end guys to stay upright. However, later designs using nylon rather
than ventile and incorporating a ridge-pole and flysheet were, and still are,
very effective.*

to decide whether the puddles forming in the corners were caused by rain coming through the seams or condensation running down them. In the end we decided on the latter. Because the temperature difference between inside and outside is less in a tent than it is in clothing, the transmission of water vapour through the gore-tex membrane is not as efficient. The result is condensation, made worse by the difficulty of ventilating a single-skin tent if it is blowing, raining or snowing outside. In warm weather, this means puddles. In cold weather, a thick layer of hoar frost forms on

the walls to shower down whenever anyone moves. Frosting will always occur at low temperatures but it is definitely worse in gore-tex tents. Moreover, a single-skin tent is not as warm as a double-skin, with its insulating layer of warmer air trapped between flysheet and inner tent, and it lacks the bell-ends so convenient for cooking and storing gear. Given that gore-tex is not very durable, either, it is far from ideal as a tent material. Designers and manufacturers seem to be acknowledging this by using it less than they did a few years ago.

Where a single-skin is justified is in a

Fig 31   A tunnel tent and a dome in use in the Lidderwat valley, Kashmir, in early April.

two-person bivi-sack or a lightweight tent for high altitudes or winter, when rain is not a problem. However, it would be cheaper and lighter to make such a tent of unproofed nylon, or a material like clima-garde, rather than gore-tex. After all, a hundred years ago Mummery was making very successful mountain tents out of silk. At present there is not such a tent on the market, but it is quite possible that manufacturers would be prepared to make one for an expedition or to adapt an existing model to different materials.

STOVES

Generally speaking, most cooking on an expedition will be on a pressure stove. In the valleys, a wood fire is cheap, efficient and a pleasure to sit around in the evenings. Sadly, in many parts of the world deforestation is a major problem, largely caused by population growth. Wood is often no longer obtainable, and if it is, it may be badly needed by the locals. Certainly nothing but dead wood should be burnt – anywhere. Particularly in Nepal it is now necessary to supply porters with pressure stoves and fuel where formerly they would have cooked on wood.

Although primus and optimus stoves have been well tried over the years, probably the best expedition stove available in terms of weight and output of heat is the MSR X-GK. Unfortunately, although it will function on almost any fuel, it is definitely happiest on white gas (Coleman's fuel)

Fig 32   Cooking on wood costs nothing and weighs nothing but, alas, is often no longer possible.

which is easy to obtain only in North America. The MSR's cheaper, quieter but less powerful cousin, the 'Whisperlite', runs only on white gas. In the third world the fuels normally available are paraffin (kerosene) and petrol (auto gas), both of which tend to clog up the jets and pipes of pressure stoves. Paraffin is the better bet, but it is essential to filter all fuel and to prime the stove with methylated spirits or solid-fuel blocks (neither of which are easy to obtain overseas). It is possible to prime pressure stoves with paraffin but it very quickly causes blockages. On top of all this, pressure stoves tend not to function well at altitude. For Base Camp use it may well be worth buying a cheap locally-made pressure stove which will be better able to cope with local fuel and conditions. In any event, it is advisable to have a complete set of spares for each stove, plenty of prickers and a lot of patience.

Fig 33   The MSR-GK multi-fuel pressure stove.

Because of these problems, outside North America most climbers prefer gas stoves, using a butane/propane mix which is less affected by cold than butane alone, although slightly more expensive. A case of karrimat for the canister in use insulates it and helps it to work more efficiently. Another idea is to wrap a length of copper wire several times around the canister and over, or near, the flame so that it acts as a heat exchange. The trouble with gas is that airlines do not permit the canisters in personal baggage and charge a fortune for freighting them. It may sometimes be possible to send them out with one of the overland tour companies but such arrangements are always fraught with risk. In centres that see considerable quantities of expedition traffic like Kathmandu and, to a lesser extent, Skardu and Gilgit in Pakistan and Huaraz in Peru, it is often possible to buy gas left behind by other parties. Elsewhere it is not so easy, and there is not an obvious, honest solution. Because gas is always going to be expensive and often in short supply, it is standard practice to use an MSR or primus stove most of the time, despite the hassles, and save gas for bivouacs and high camps.

It goes without saying that if you carry gas canisters in you should carry them out. Yet the ubiquitous blue or orange cans are the most widespread form of climbing pollution. From Kenya to the Himalaya, from Greenland to Patagonia, piles of them accumulate in otherwise wild and beautiful places. It is all too easy to assume that because a heap of garbage is already there, a little more will make no difference. But it does make a difference, and it is precisely that attitude that is the root of the problem. It is better by far to expect to carry out not only our own rubbish, but at least some of other people's as well. If such an attitude

was to become widely accepted, there would soon be no problem.

A stove system that can be hung from the roof of the tent is a good idea. It keeps the fuel container off the snow, shields the flame from the wind, and ensures that the pot cannot be knocked over, all in one. Such systems have been improvised by climbers for years but they can now be bought. Failing that, an insulated base for the stove makes life a lot easier; otherwise, a hot stove swiftly melts its way downwards and if the pot does not tip over first, lack of oxygen puts it out. A piece of karrimat or plywood wrapped around with aluminium foil serves well. Less effective is a flat shovel or a deadman. A windshield of aluminium sheet, like that supplied with an MSR, is worthwhile for any stove.

POTS AND PANS

Useful for the valleys and at Base Camp and obtainable locally are: a hurricane lamp or candles, large cooking pots and lids, a frying pan, a pressure cooker, a sharp knife for cutting up vegetables, a fish-slice for turning pancakes over, a long wooden spoon, and, if you like chapattis, a rolling-pin. These are all luxuries that may have to be sacrificed in the interests of weight. A pan scourer is often forgotten but makes life much easier.

On the mountain, two pots, both with lids, are handy, plus a bowl, large mug and spoon each. A Swiss Army knife has a host of uses. On bivis the weight can be cut down further by taking only one pot, one mug, and a spoon each.

SHOVELS, SKIS, SLEDGES

Shovels are a must in Alaska and other heavily glaciated regions where snow caves are a norm and shelter walls for tents advisable. Elsewhere, the higher the altitude and the earlier or later the season the more useful they will be, although they are not essential unless you are intending to snow cave. The best shovels have a large flat metal blade with a short, detachable handle.

Skis or snow-shoes are an essential in all seasons in Alaska and northern Greenland, not only because they make travel in soft snow so much easier and faster, but because they are a significant safety factor on crevassed glaciers. In other parts of the world their weight usually precludes carry-

Fig 34   A useful shovel with detachable handle and broad, strong blade.

Fig 35   In deep snow skis rule, OK?!

ing them long distances for use on only short sections of the route. Snow-shoes are definitely second-best, unless you have to carry them over the mountain for use on the far side. Ski descents have been made of a number of big peaks, including Cho Oyu, Noshaq, Mustagh Ata, Aconcagua and McKinley, although both carrying the skis and the actual skiing are exhausting at altitude, with the chances of a fatal slip increased. By contrast, a winter or spring ski journey, taking in easy peaks, is a very rewarding form of mountaineering that can be enjoyed by anyone anywhere in the world. It is, however, very strenuous as all food and equipment have to be carried.

Skis can be either nordic (long and thin) or alpine (shorter and broader). Nordic skis are light and faster on easy terrain. Alpine skis are much heavier but easier to handle on steep or icy slopes as the heels can be clamped down. Bindings for nordic skis use a three-pin or cable system neither of which will work with a plastic climbing boot. However, the Ramer binding and the Emery Medium are both systems that enable a plastic boot to be fitted to a nordic ski. For a long journey, bendy leather double-boots and ordinary bindings are more comfortable. Not all alpine touring bindings will take a climbing boot; among those that do are the Silvretta, Salewa and Fritschi. For most mountain use, whether you are using nordic or alpine skis, you will need a pair of 'skins' that stick on to the sole of the ski and enable you to walk uphill. For more details about ski mountaineering equipment consult Martyn Hurn, *Skiing Real Snow* (Crowood Press 1987), or Peter Cliff, *Ski Mountaineering* (Unwin Hyman 1987).

Ski sticks are very useful even if skis are not being used. They serve as walking sticks when carrying heavy loads over unstable

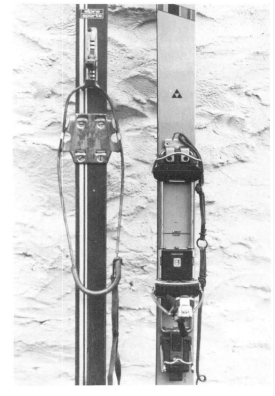

Fig 36   A nordic mountain ski fitted with a cable binding (left), and an alpine touring ski with Silvretta binding (right).

moraine and are a support when climbing easy-angled snow at altitude. They can also be used as crevasse probes (especially the type that can be screwed together, with removable baskets), and as tent pegs (ordinary pegs are not worth carrying on snow).

Long bamboo wands, too, fulfil different roles. They can be used to mark a complex route on a glacier, to identify a snow cave or cache of food and, like ski sticks, to probe for crevasses and hold the tent down on snow.

Fig 37 A nordic ski boot with felt inner. An overgaiter is important to keep the leather dry – if it gets wet in the mountains, it may never dry out.

Fig 38 A plastic climbing boot in a touring binding. Not all bindings will take a climbing boot.

Fig 39   Mike Browne fitting skins to nordic mountain skis.

Sledges are widely used in North America, Scandinavia and the Arctic as a way of transporting loads that are too heavy to be carried. Climbers in Alaska frequently use a child's plastic toboggan bought in a super-market. For long journeys, however, it is worth having a purpose-made 'pulk' which has light wooden shafts so that you cannot be run down by the sledge, a weather-proof cover and straps for securing the load. Sledges of either sort are most effective on hard, smooth surfaces and are at their worst on traverses and sastrugi (wind-eroded waves of frozen snow).

SPARES AND REPAIRS

How much you take in the way of spares – ice-axe, crampons, rope and so on – will depend on the scale of the trip. If transport to and from the mountain seems assured, or is going to be essential anyway, it makes

Fig 40   Rod Brown harnessed to a Swedish-made pulk in Greenland. On a firm surface like this it is possible to drag 200lb or more.

sense to have some spares. But if you really want to be lightweight or hope to walk out unaided, you will have to take a chance on it. Nine times out of ten you will get away with it, and the tenth time you will find a way round the problem. Where there's a will there's a way ...

Do take a small repair kit though, however lightweight you aim to be. Useful items are:

Swiss Army penknife
Needles and thread
Sailmaker's needle and palm
Super-glue
Araldite
Nylon patches and adhesive
Pop-rivets
Wire
Parachute cord
Waterproof tape
Spare crampon bar, screws and nuts
Crampon spanner and/or allan key

RADIOS

Radios are a bone of contention. On the one hand, they can be invaluable to maintain contact between Base Camp and climbers on the mountain, or between camps, and for that reason are regarded as essential on large expeditions employing siege tactics. Even on small expeditions, lack of communication can cause confusion if the climbers split up; for example, a pair coming up expecting to use a tent may find it occupied. On the other hand, even walkie-talkies are expensive to buy, extra weight to carry and liable not to work when they are most needed. A radio powerful enough to contact the outside world will be beyond the means of most lightweight expeditions.

A voice over the radio can be a comfort in a remote situation, but it can also create a misplaced sense of security. The eight Russian women who died on Pic Lenin in the Pamirs in 1974 were in radio contact with their encouraging Master of Sport to the very end, and one is left with the inescapable feeling that without his voice they would have turned back early enough to descend safely. Even Joe Tasker, Pete Boardman and Dick Renshaw were not immune to this insidious influence. Having decided, after their successful ascent of Kangchenjunga, that radios would have been useful, they bought some for their attempt on K2. High on the mountain, in dubious weather, they were urged on by their well-meaning liaison officer, with an optimistic forecast that lured them upward into a storm in which they nearly died. Had they trusted their own judgement, the whole epic would have been avoided (Joe Tasker, *Savage Arena* (Methuen 1982)).

The nub of the matter, however, is that radios reduce the element of adventure. They are a link to the world below, a psychological prop which is at once reassuring and reduces the sense of commitment that is so important on a small expedition. The idea of a personal venture into the unknown, an insistence on self-reliance, and the taking of carefully-calculated risks by individuals, and living with the consequences, are at the root of mountaineering. The large expedition has, to a large extent, left such values behind. In view of the money involved, it is necessarily about publicity before, during and after the climb, the promotion of both climbers and sponsors, complicated logistics, and teamwork co-ordinated by a leader. Computers are useful, and radios essential to the careful orchestrating of the whole performance.

But if the style of an ascent is more important than success for personal satisfaction, as many believe, radios are out.

If you want to be certain of a speedy rescue, it would be better to stay in the Alps, for in third-world countries, even with a radio, it is not simply a question of calling in a helicopter. Any accident will involve a painful evacuation and/or a lengthy wait for outside help.

In this context, Joe Simpson's account of his epic descent from Siula Grande in the Andes with Simon Yates, after breaking his leg high on the mountain, makes sobering reading (*Touching the Void*, Jonathan Cape 1988).

3 Travel

I read recently in one of the Sunday papers a letter complaining bitterly about Gatwick Airport. Although the writer and his wife travel regularly all over the world, they were so exhausted by the walk from the aeroplane to the terminus that they had to be rescued by airline officials with wheelchairs. I could not help but think of Tilman's remarks about air travel:

'Instead of saying that I travelled to Shanghai by air I should prefer to say I was carried there; for it seems to me time to draw a hard and fast line between travellers and passengers. A journey of many thousands of miles by air and bus . . . without the least physical effort on my part and with a despicably small increase in knowledge as a result, can hardly be called travelling. To my mind two distinguishing marks of a traveller are that he exerts himself and that he moves slowly . . . while a passenger moves swiftly by machinery.' H. W. Tilman, *China to Chitral* (C.U. Press 1951).

Tilman's distinction is even more valid today than it was forty years ago. In more and more places, including the Himalaya, the opportunity exists to be carried as a passenger farther and farther into the mountains; indeed, skiers like to be taken right to the top of them. Yet, even if that gives us more time to devote to climbing (or skiing), we are the losers in the long run. There is so much to be seen, learned and enjoyed about any mountain on the journey to it. There is more to mountains than climbing . . .

THE INITIAL JOURNEY

An expedition, lightweight or otherwise, usually means an initial journey by air. True, climbers from the 'lower 48' can take the long road north through Canada to Alaska, but the even longer journey south to the Andes has been made hazardous by the war in Nicaragua. The overland journey from Europe to India that was so popular with small expeditions in the 1960s and 70s, has been made difficult, and at times impossible, by the turmoil in Afghanistan and Iran. At present the southern route from Iran into Pakistan is open, but it is not an easy journey.

An appealing option is to sail to your destination. Tilman was an early protagonist of this approach to mountains, taking first *Mischief* and later *Sea Breeze* and *Baroque* to many different parts of the Arctic, Antarctica and Patagonia. If you have to buy or charter a boat it is prohibitively expensive, but if you already own one or know someone who owns a boat sturdy enough, the journey becomes an adventure in its own right. On Tilman's voyages the mountain objectives often proved something of an anti-climax after all that had gone before. This is probably the only way a lightweight expedition can visit Antarctica. (A party of six from New Zealand, one of whom owned a boat, recently climbed on Smith Island for only NZ $3,000 a head – about £1,200.)

Most people, however, will have to fly, with all the restrictions on bulk and weight that implies. A definite advantage of flying

Fig 41   Porters crossing the Marsyandi River in Nepal.

Fig 42   The overland route to India passing through the deserts of Iran and Afghanistan was very popular in the 1960s and 70s.

Fig 43   If you can beg, borrow or steal a boat, it is an exciting way to approach the mountains.

to North and most parts of South America is that you are restricted only to two pieces of baggage rather than to a certain weight. This means that the only real problem is obtaining, or making, bags large enough to contain everything. Elsewhere, unless you travel First Class, there is a weight restriction of 20kg per passenger – a definite handicap however lightweight you are attempting to be. The airline will usually turn a blind eye to 2 or 3kg, but excess baggage charges, once they are imposed, are appallingly high – one per cent of the First Class fare per kilo, which is £11 a kilo on a flight to India. It is worth contacting the airline beforehand. It is unlikely that you will be given free tickets, but you may well obtain a concession on the baggage allowance. If you are carrying skis this is especially important. The trouble is that you may have to travel at a standard fare rather than at a bucket-shop price.

Failing that, climbers have to resort to the time-honoured expedient of wearing as

Fig 44   Giant kit-bags are useful for air travel when there is no weight restriction.

much as possible, and stuffing pockets with hardware. It is worth having some carrier bags into which you can put all the surplus clothing once you are on the aircraft, and bringing some sandals to put on your feet. Emerging at Dubai or Rawalpindi in plastic boots, gaiters, overtrousers and down jacket is beyond a joke. Do not be tempted to carry a large piece of hand baggage: it will almost certainly be weighed as well. You will usually get away with a small day-pack, preferably on your back where it is clearly visible and does not have to be asked for. Needless to say, small does not mean light. If the airline is making a point of weighing *all* hand baggage, a less honest alternative is simply to leave your bag with a friend round the corner or in the cafeteria until you have checked in. This subterfuge is not totally

reprehensible when you consider that your body weight will be well below that of many passengers. Ice-axes and hammers are not worth carrying in your hand baggage, despite their weight. They will be found at the security check and regarded as dangerous weapons to be taken away and carried separately on the aircraft (even a Swiss Army knife can suffer this fate). They are returned at the end of the journey, but there is always a chance that they will go astray, particularly if you change aircraft. It is just one more hassle that you can do without.

When you pass through customs there is no harm in explaining that you are going mountaineering or trekking, but it is safer to avoid the word expedition, as it may entail a whole new set of regulations and procedures. You are unlikely to be carrying much food but it is diplomatic not to mention it unless specifically asked.

Sending your baggage ahead by air-freight is not to be recommended. It may sound straightforward enough to go to the freight department, find your bags and see them through customs but, in the East at any rate, it is far from simple. You may never find the baggage. If you do, you will probably make several journeys to the airport before you find the right man in the right office at the right time to release it. Finally, clearing it through customs is liable to become suddenly exceedingly complicated and possibly expensive. You have been warned!

THE APPROACH

Mechanical transport

In North America and the Arctic ski-planes, float-planes, helicopters, ships and inflat-

Fig 45   The retractable skis, first developed in New Zealand in the 1950s, that revolutionized the use of aircraft in mountains.

Fig 46   The Twin Otter is widely used in Antarctica, Greenland and Arctic Canada.

Fig 47 Helicopters are now in common use all over the world, but they are always expensive to hire.

ables are all used for access in different places. All have novelty value for climbers from Europe and can be part of the adventure. Distances are so huge that light aircraft are regarded and handled rather like cars, and are widely used by climbers not just for access but to lay depots or for re-supply in the middle of a trip. They are prohibited from landing within most National Parks, however. If relying on a pick-up by aircraft (or boat, come to that), plenty of food and fuel in reserve is essential in case of delay. To avoid these lengthy waits and to save money, climbers in Alaska and the Yukon have sometimes chosen to float down a river on small inflatable rafts. Another attractive possibility, for those with time to travel through the country rather than just

climb a mountain, is to use dog-team support for some or all of the journey. With the exception of rafting, none of these forms of transport come cheaply, however. Addresses for air taxis and dog-teams in the Alaska Range are given in the Appendix.

Although the Swiss used an aircraft to 5,500 metres on Dhaulagiri in 1960 (and crashed it!) the idea never caught on in Himalayan climbing – more, one suspects, because of expense than from ethical considerations. The introduction of heli-skiing in Kashmir may herald a change, in which machines will be used more and more to go higher and higher. One hopes not, but it is probably inevitable. Fortunately, the effects of altitude will always act as a constraint.

Fig 48   *Rafting down-river after a climb on the Lotus-flower Tower in Canada.*

Fig 49   *Using dogs in Alaska. Note the small size of the sledge, indicating that this team is more used to joy-rides or racing than to pulling a heavy load.*

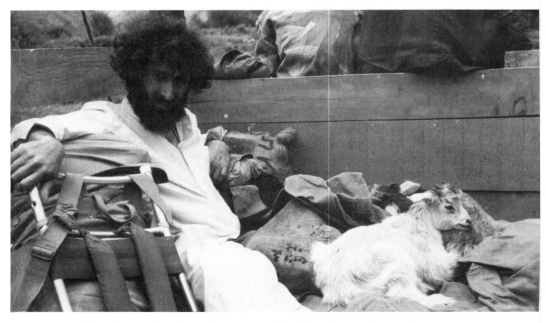

Fig 50   *Geoff Cohen settling down for an uncomfortable ride in the back of a lorry.*

Fig 51   Local buses are an experience in themselves . . .

Meanwhile, roads built for military reasons snake their way up increasing numbers of Himalayan valleys, making access cheaper and quicker but replacing beautiful walks with hot, uncomfortable rides by jeep, bus or lorry. Nevertheless, a bus ride in India or Nepal is a memorable experience for its own sake, a chance to live like the locals for a while . . .

Porters and pack-animals

The traditional picture of an expedition is of a long line of porters winding its way through the hills. In fact, in many parts of the Himalaya and in Iran, Turkey and South America, pack-animals – donkeys, mules or ponies – are more common as a form of transport. Either way, porters or pony-men

will have very clear ideas about how far they wish to travel each day and where they wish to stop for the night. Usually there will be established stages, and even if they are not as far as you would like, it will only cause trouble if you insist on going further. Clearly, more days mean more money, so sometimes the porters or drivers will try to pull a fast one. A liaison officer can prove his worth (or otherwise) here, but it is worth asking around anyway to discover the normal length of the journey.

The same applies to prices. In theory, these are regulated by the government in the Himalayan countries, but in less-frequented areas it may be necessary to bargain. There will always be one rate for locals and another for foreigners, but for the sake of other parties as well as your own pocket, it

73

Fig 52   Donkeys are the commonest beast of burden throughout the third world.

Fig 53   Not surprisingly, owners of ponies do not hire them out without a driver.

Fig 54   Powerful but slow, yaks are the heavy-goods vehicles of the mountains.

is sensible not to accept the first figure quoted. A spring-balance is useful to keep everybody happy about the weight being carried. Loads vary from place to place, but usually a porter will carry 25kg. A donkey will carry slightly more, a mule twice as much and a pony somewhere in between. Yaks are the heavy goods vehicles of the mountains – they will carry 60kg or more but are very slow. They are also recalcitrant beasts, which is why hybrids called dzos are more commonly used.

A knowledge of the local *lingua franca* is obviously invaluable, and even a few words make a big difference and more than repay the effort made to learn them. Nevertheless, mime works surprisingly well if need be. It

is unusual not to meet someone who speaks good English and his or her friendship is worth cultivating.

If the details of the walk-in can be amicably arranged at the outset, then you can relax and enjoy it. The walk is a chance to get fit and to acclimatize, not just to increasing altitude, but to the culture and customs of the land you are passing through. If the budget is not too tight, it is infinitely preferable to carry only a light day-sack and enjoy to the full the strange sights, sounds and smells surrounding you. There will be plenty of opportunities to hump big loads later on. As for Sherpas or high-altitude porters, they are neither necessary nor desirable for a lightweight expedition.

Fig 55   Allocating loads is usually a protracted affair. A spring-balance helps to settle arguments.

Although it is arguable that using Sherpas above the snow-line is no different to using porters below it, the fact remains that you will no longer be a small party, they will require a lot of extra clothing and equipment, and the cost of paying them will greatly increase the cost of the trip. Above all, you are no longer climbing the mountain by your own efforts.

Remember that the people you employ will be no better and no worse in their attitude to work and their employer than people anywhere else in the world. Nor need you feel guilty that you are paying them a pittance, for it is a fair wage in terms of the local economy and what it will buy. Some people will work their hearts out, others will do as little as possible. Some will be as honest as the day is long, others will lose no opportunity to take advantage of

you or create trouble. So do not be surprised if the porters go on strike, or small items mysteriously go missing. Bakhsheesh, in the form of cigarettes or sugar, helps to keep relations cordial; sometimes it is expected. I have many happy memories of sitting round camp-fires with porters and pony-men, of sharing food and helping and being helped in awkward places. But as a cautionary tale I quote from an article in the *Alpine Journal* I wrote some years ago about a two-man expedition in the Western Karakoram:

'Having crossed the moraine-covered snout of the Baltar Glacier in a long detour enforced by an unfordable river, and returned to the stony wastes of the main valley, we reached, about midday, the place called Toltar. There was nothing there but a few charred sticks and some dry-stone

Fig 56   Porters on the move in Nepal.

walling beneath a boulder. But the coolies had made it clear that Toltar was the day's objective, so we sat down to wait for them.

'They never came. Every hour or so we carefully scanned the valley with binoculars but there was never a sign of them. Dick read Richard Burton on Sindh. Having rashly left my book behind in the interests of weight, I contemplated, alternately, the sky and my navel. The hours passed and we began to feel hungry. Finally, as evening drew in, we unrolled our sleeping bags and tried unsuccessfully to stave off the pangs in sleep. Just before dark, Dick had a final look round but still there was nothing to be seen, not even the smoke of a fire.

'Next morning our hunger was no less, but convinced that the porters must be nearby, we left our sacks and back-tracked a mile or so, searching and shouting. We were certain that they could not have passed us. Not only were we keeping a look-out, but at that point there is so little room between the mountainside and the river that they could hardly help but see us. But there was neither sight nor sound of the two men. With nothing to eat, there was no alternative but to beat a retreat to Bar, by now a highly desirable land flowing with chapattis and salt tea.

'At the insistence of the villagers who professed themselves certain that the porters would return any moment, we spent two days in Bar, lying in the shade of a walnut tree. An almost morbid fear of the police stemmed, we learned later, from a successful raid in search of stolen property only a fortnight before. So strong was this fear that it induced the local prophet to go into a convulsive trance, wherein he was bold enough to foretell the very hour of the porters' arrival. Unfortunately, he was wrong. In the meantime, we lived on what the villagers chose to provide, mostly mulberries and chapatties of mature vintage, sometimes eggs and, on one memorable occasion, a packet of vermicelli, a tin of cheese and a large quantity of sugar boiled up together into an edible glue. However, two days seems a very long time when one is a public spectacle throughout the hours of daylight and has nothing to do but debate the likelihood of villainy or disaster. Eventually, when requests that we should stay showed signs of hardening into a refusal to let us leave, we flitted on a dark moonless night to Chalt – our noiseless departure marred only by Dick describing a somersault from one terraced field to the next wrenching a knee in the process. In Chalt we made a statement to the Inspector of Police and, after a day of over-indulging in apricots and sweet biscuits, returned to Gilgit full of gloom.

'With a damaged knee and his holiday almost over, Dick cut short the fiasco of our "expedition" by taking the first available flight back to Rawalpindi. Within minutes of his departure I met a policeman from Chalt in the bazaar and learned that our

Fig 57   This porter could not have been more cheerful and hard-working, despite a load of skis which meant shuffling sideways for long sections of the route.

Fig 58   This porter was of a less friendly disposition – I never did see him smile.

baggage had been recovered. Back in Chalt, I was told that the coolies had brought it in themselves, claiming to have carried it all the way to the Kukuay glacier and back and demanding nine days' wages for their pains. Unfortunately the Inspector believed them. Apparently one of them had made the pilgrimage to Mecca and "They are very gentle men". Secretly, I wondered if a man who had been to Mecca might not be all the more anxious to con an infidel. Aloud, I voiced the suspicion that they might have spent most of those days reclining in the shade of a birch grove nearer home with some goatherds. But there was no convincing the Inspector and it is no easier to argue with the Law in Pakistan than anywhere else. Reluctantly I handed over the money.'

'A Summer in Gilgit', *Alpine Journal* 1977

THE WALK-IN
Food and Drink

'One point to which I must draw attention, and which is the most important of all for the explorer of the Himalaya and especially for the mountaineer – that is to have a really dependable digestion' (C. G. Bruce, *Himalayan Wanderer*, Alexander Maclehose 1934).

Thus spoke General Bruce many years ago, but his words are no less true today than they were then. I remember seeing the same thought expressed rather differently on the toilet wall of one of Kathmandu's many cafes:

'If the bottom has dropped out of your world eat at Joe's
and the world will drop out of your bottom.'

Few expeditions to South America or the East will escape without a 'dose of the trots' somewhere along the way. Often it is caused by no more than a bumpy bus ride or unfamiliar food and, though unpleasant, it can be shaken off in a day or two with the help of Lomotil or Imodium. There is a school of thought that says it is better not to use drugs that reduce the number of bowel movements without treating the cause. On the other hand, if there is anything more miserable than diarrhoea on a long bus journey it is repeated journeys out into the wind and snow in the middle of the night.

More serious are the various forms of dysentery that will linger on for weeks if not treated with the right medicines. Giardiasis (characterized by 'eggy burps') and amebiasis (in which the diarrhoea is mild but persistent and accompanied by fever, tiredness and pains in muscles and joints) are both caused by protozoa and can be treated with Flagyl (Metronidazole). It is recommended that this is followed by a course of Furamide to kill off the cysts that may have been left behind, otherwise the condition may recur. It is dangerous to take alcohol while on these drugs. Bacillary dysentery (caused by bacteria and usually identified by severe stomach cramps, vomiting and pus and blood in the stools) needs to be treated with broad-spectrum antibiotics. It is not always easy for the layman to differentiate between these types of dysentery, although correct diagnosis is obviously important for treatment. Dehydration easily becomes a serious problem so it is vital to take plenty of fluids. If vomiting makes this difficult, Maxolon can help; it will also reduce stomach cramp.

Even nastier, however, is hepatitis. Three different types of virus infection are recognized at present, of which two can cause chronic liver disease and death. Fortunately, mountaineers are most at risk from hepatitis A, the least virulent of the three, which is spread in dirty food and water. It manifests itself first as a loss of appetite and lethargy, and can, but does not always, progress to fever, nausea, aching joints and jaundice (yellowing of the whites of the eyes and of the skin). It lasts from three to six weeks, but the debilitating effects can linger for months. There is no specific treatment for hepatitis, but the chance of contracting it can be reduced, though not eliminated, by a shot of gamma globulin.

As with all medical problems, prevention is far better than cure. All these diseases are caused by dirty water or dirty food, and can be avoided by taking a few precautions – with luck. Suspect all water until really high in the mountains. The jug of water on the table in a restaurant may or may not be safe. The clear, tinkling stream, crying out to be drunk, may be descending from a village hidden high above where it has been used for every conceivable human and animal activity; or there may be a goatherds' encampment round the next bend in the path. Iodine tablets are the most effective and convenient way of sterilizing water, although iodine can be harmful if taken regularly for months rather than weeks. Most water-purifying tablets are chlorine-based, killing off bacteria but not the protozoa like giardia and amoeba. Boiling water is an option, but to be completely safe it needs to be boiled for at least ten minutes at sea-level, with an extra minute for every 300 metres of altitude. Iodine tablets and a range of portable filters are available from Survival Aids Ltd, Morland, Penrith, Cumbria, UK Tel: 0800 262752.

Human faeces are the major cause of polluted water, so it is important not to compound the problem with your own. If there is a toilet, use it, however unsavoury it looks and smells. If excreting on the trail, never do so near running water and preferably bury the faeces a few inches down where there are plenty of bacteria in the soil to get to work on it. If you have to leave it on the surface, at least carry a lighter or matches and burn your toilet paper to prevent it blowing around or adding to the proliferation of 'pink flowers' that spring up beside popular trekking routes.

Fruit and vegetables are the other trouble-makers, and should always be peeled or thoroughly washed in clean water. Avoid salads in restaurants; you may be maligning them but it is better to be safe than sorry. In general, if food is hot and has been freshly cooked it should be safe. The exception is meat which goes 'off' very quickly in hot countries without refrigeration yet, being expensive, is often used when it should have been thrown away. On the whole, it is wise to leave chang and other local beverages for the walk-out, when you can either celebrate or drown your sorrows. The hot sweet tea of the chai-shops is usually fine, however, and a good way of replacing calories as well as fluid. Always try to wash your hands before meals and wash up afterwards in hot water.

Turbid grey glacier water is full of particles of mica and other minerals held in suspension, which irritate the lining of the stomach and can cause diarrhoea if the water is drunk in quantity. A few mouthfuls does no harm, but if nothing else is available for cooking, it is wise to leave it to stand for as long as possible first so that a sediment forms.

If you do not take salt in your food normally it is worth doing so in hot countries where so much is lost in sweat. In

Fig 59   The dim, smoky interior of a typical chai-shop.

Fig 60   Breakfast on a high alp during an approach march in Kulu.

very dry, hot regions, like the Hindu Kush and the Karakoram, heat stroke is a real possibility. This is nearly always linked with dehydration so drink plenty. Fruit crystals are a good idea to take away the taste of iodine or chlorine in water-purifying tablets. An early start and afternoon siesta is a sensible routine to adopt: 'Only mad dogs and Englishmen go out in the midday sun . . .'

Although in some Nepalese valleys it is possible to buy food and meals along the way, they are the exceptions rather than the rule. It is safer to be totally self-sufficient and regard it as a bonus if you are invited into someone's house or find you can buy eggs, potatoes or whatever. It is unfair to expect villagers to sell you food that may already be in short supply.

Clothing

In hot countries, light loose-fitting cotton clothes will be the most comfortable. It pays to see what the locals wear and even to have some clothes made up by a local tailor. Shorts and T-shirts are not very versatile, by turns too cold and not offering enough protection from the sun. Garments like pyjamas with legs and sleeves that can be rolled up and down at will, are more practical. Light trainers are the best foot-wear. Boots are not usually necessary until the snow-line or moraines are reached, and are liable to cause blisters in the heat. The exception is in monsoon conditions when light boots and gore-tex waterproofs are more appropriate. A sun hat or peaked cap is often useful. Some use umbrellas to keep off sun as well as rain. People with contact

Fig 61   Des Rubens wearing a practical cotton suit made for him in Afghanistan.

Fig 62   Sun hat and shades – essential items of kit in the mid-summer heat of the Hindu Kush or Karakoram.

lenses find dust a problem, particularly in big open valleys prone to wind; keep a pair of goggles handy, just in case.

Sun cream and lip salve may be necessary long before the snow-line. In the lower valleys, a sleeping bag may be too warm, but a sheet liner will keep off the mosquitoes and creepy-crawlies. Accepting hospitality and staying in local 'hotels' is part of the fun of travelling, but the consequences are sometimes irritating. A supply of flea powder can be worth its weight in gold . . .

RIVER CROSSING

Crossing rivers is one of the greatest hazards of climbing in big mountains. This is particularly true for climbers from Britain and Europe who at home only occasionally do not have the option of using a bridge. Many climbers are not aware of the formidable power of moving water and do not treat rivers with the respect they deserve. I speak from experience!

On one occasion, in Kulu, I nearly drowned when I rashly chose to attempt a crossing just upstream of a submerged log, thinking it might offer support. Instead, the force of the water pressed me against it and the pole I was using as a 'third leg' jammed in such a way that it pinned my leg immovably under the log. For what felt like several minutes, but was probably only a few seconds, I was quite helpless, swallowing a lot of water in my attempts to breathe as waves washed over me. Although I was on a rope and my wife and friends were on the bank only a few feet away, there was nothing they could do. In the end, desperation gave me strength and I was able to wrench the pole free, but I have had a healthy respect for rivers ever since (a respect that was heightened rather than lessened after I took up canoeing). I felt even more chastened when we discovered, only three hundred yards upstream, a couple of logs thrown across the river as a makeshift bridge by local shepherds. Impetuosity had nearly ended in disaster. Anybody planning an expedition for the first time would be well advised not just to read this chapter, but to practise thoroughly the different techniques that can make river crossings safer. They will never be totally safe, yet they are often unavoidable.

Young rivers, high in the mountains, are

Fig 63   Porters crossing a river in Nepal. River crossings are always potentially dangerous but often unavoidable.

*Fig 64   Shallow but fast-flowing streams should not be underestimated –
they can be just as awkward as deeper slow-moving water.*

steep, fast-flowing and rocky, but relatively narrow and they can often be crossed by boulder-hopping. Be wary of leaping on to wet rocks with a big pack – they will nearly always be slippery and the weight affects your balance. Often it is better to avoid the obvious flat surfaces and make for the joint where two boulders lie side by side, even if it does mean putting your foot in the water. As long as you do not linger, gaiters will keep the water out of your boots. If in doubt it is worth a thorough search up and down stream for a natural rock bridge or a fallen tree.

Slow-moving rivers and deep pools are not so common, but if they are encountered on the approach to the mountains, it is perfectly feasible to swim across, pushing your sack in front of you or even lying on top of it. If you have a strong plastic bag inside, well sealed at the top, it will not only keep the contents dry, but enable the sack to float. A 'swan's neck' is a good way to seal the top: fold the plastic bag into a series of pleats so it forms a thin neck, then double it over and tie firmly with a piece of string or a handkerchief.

However, it is the glacier rivers that are too wide and deep to be boulder-hopped and too fast to be swum that are the usual problem for the mountaineer. There are three factors to be considered: when, where, and how to cross them.

When to Cross

Even insignificant little trickles can become raging torrents after heavy rain, and in spate conditions there may be no choice but to wait for the level to drop. The smaller the river, the faster it will rise and fall. In winter, glacier streams will not be much of a problem. Snowfall and avalanches bury them in places, and sometimes they freeze over giving access to gorges that are impassable in summer. In summer, however, they are a major obstacle. The safest time to attempt a crossing is early in the morning when glacial melt is at its lowest. Once the sun comes up the water-level can rise dramatically.

Where to Cross

Common sense is the best guide here. Ask yourself 'What will happen if... ?' A waterfall or major rapid immediately downstream, steep banks, and trees in the water or overhanging it are not to be recommended. Where the river is broadest it will also be shallowest. Often the best crossing places are where it becomes braided, splitting up into several channels.

How to Cross

Keep your boots on. They make it much easier to gain a purchase on a slippery or moving bottom. Undo the waistbelt (and chest-strap, if you use one) of your pack, just in case... Keep clothing to a minimum and wear waterproofs on top. Melt water is going to be *very* cold, but you want something dry to put on the other side. Make sure your spare clothing is inside a sealed plastic bag. Do not underestimate shallow but fast-flowing streams. Speed is as significant as depth, and knee-deep water that is swiftly flowing may be harder to negotiate than slower-moving water up to the thighs.

On your own

Face upstream or across the river, but never downstream – the current causes your knees

Fig 65   Using a strong stick as a 'third leg'.

to buckle. (Some New Zealanders advocate running downstream but such a dynamic approach is difficult with a big pack.) A good strong pole about six feet long is a great help if you can find one, placed well upstream for support while you move your feet sideways (Fig 65). Accept that the current is going to make it difficult to go directly across the river and aim for a point diagonally downstream.

Linked arms

Any number from two upwards can gain mutual support by linking arms as shown in Fig 66. The heaviest or strongest person is best at the upstream end where he or she can bear the brunt of the current.

Fig 66   Linking arms for support. The largest members of the party are on the left, bearing the brunt of the current.

Fig 67   Arms over shoulders, hands grasping pack straps. A good method for people of the same height.

Linked straps

A stronger method for people of similar height is to cross arms over the shoulders and hold the further shoulder-strap on the pack of the person(s) next to you (Fig 67).

Huddle

An alternative for three people is to grasp each other's pack straps, with one person facing upstream and the other two facing each other (Fig 68). The drawback to this is that one person has to walk backwards, but for a group of three it is probably stronger than the previous two methods.

Fig 68   The huddle – good for a threesome.

Fig 69   Using a pole for mutual support.

*Fig 70   A log is the best of all – you can even swim with it if need be –
but not always available when you want it.*

Pole

Link arms, then grasp a strong pole with both hands (Fig 69). This method was developed hundreds of years ago by the Maoris for crossing the many fast-flowing rivers of New Zealand. It is probably the most effective of the methods described, except on a very uneven river bed where the lack of flexibility creates problems. If need be, it is possible to use tent-poles by taping the joints and then taping several poles together.

Log

In very deep water a log may be more effective than a pole as it gives extra buoyancy. Here you hold the log rather than each other, one arm over it, the other under, as shown in Fig 70. In many mountain areas, however, it will be difficult to find a log of the right shape and size.

Emergencies

If you get part of the way across and decide that the crossing is not feasible or too hazardous, the best course is simply to walk backwards. Attempting to wheel around in mid-stream to face the right way is risky.

If you are unlucky enough to be swept away, lie on your back with your feet downstream (Fig 71); that way, you are least vulnerable, you can see where you are going and you can maybe fend off rocks with your feet. It is worth keeping your pack on, initially, as it provides buoyancy and protection. Push down with your thumb at the bottom of one of the shoulder straps to prevent the pack riding over your head. Kicking with your feet and using the other arm in a side-stroke make for the bank,

Fig 71 The swimmer is floating on his back, facing downstream, supported by the buoyancy of his pack which is lined with a well-sealed plastic bag.

looking out for eddies of quiet water. If the pack does ride up, slip it off but keep hold of it with one hand. It is still useful for buoyancy, as well as containing equipment you cannot afford to lose.

Using a Rope

If all else fails, a rope can be used to cross, provided the river is not too wide. One way is to make a continuous loop of rope by tying the two ends together (often it will be necessary to tie two ropes together to get sufficient length). The first person to cross steps into a loop formed with an overhand or figure-of-eight knot; if the loop is kept fairly slack it would be possible to escape from it in an emergency. As he crosses he is pulling out a doubled rope. From one, held by a belayer upstream (Fig 72) he can receive tension, which helps considerably. However, if he slips it is unlikely that he will be able to regain his feet and a tight rope will pull him underwater. It is important, therefore, that neither belayer nor rope are

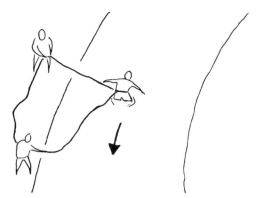

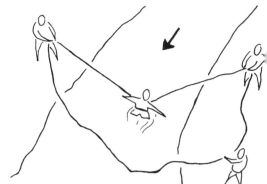

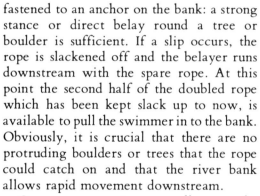

Fig 72   Using a rope. The person crossing can take support from the upstream rope, but if need be can be hauled ashore downstream.

Fig 73   Once one person is across, support can be given from both sides of the river, although the slack rope downstream needs to be managed to reduce drag.

fastened to an anchor on the bank: a strong stance or direct belay round a tree or boulder is sufficient. If a slip occurs, the rope is slackened off and the belayer runs downstream with the spare rope. At this point the second half of the doubled rope which has been kept slack up to now, is available to pull the swimmer in to the bank. Obviously, it is crucial that there are no protruding boulders or trees that the rope could catch on and that the river bank allows rapid movement downstream.

Once one person is across, all except the last can cross with the support of two ropes, one from either bank (Fig 73). If anyone slips in that situation, the same principles apply. Both ropes must be slackened off, and the swimmer hauled ashore, across the current rather than against it, to the nearest bank. This will involve some running on the part of the belayers. The last person crosses in the same manner as the first.

An alternative, once one person is across, is to stretch a handline diagonally downstream across the river. Ideally the anchors

should be high and the rope tensioned so that anyone slipping will not be dragged underwater. Each person, as he crosses, is clipped into the handline with a sling and can gain some support from it. He is also tied in to the middle of a second rope, so that he can be hauled across in either direction if need be. This is important as otherwise he could be left stranded in mid-stream.

Tyrolean Traverse

A modification of the handline is the Tyrolean Traverse on which gear can be hauled across and climbers (once one person is across) can stay dry-shod. To be successful this depends on having the rope high and well-tensioned (Figs 74, 75 and 76). Unless you are into the Commando Crawl (Fig 77) – not as precarious as it looks, but not exactly comfortable – hanging under the rope in a harness is the way to do it (Fig 78). A Tyrolean Traverse imposes severe forces on both anchors and rope; if 8mm or 9mm ropes are being used it is wise to double up.

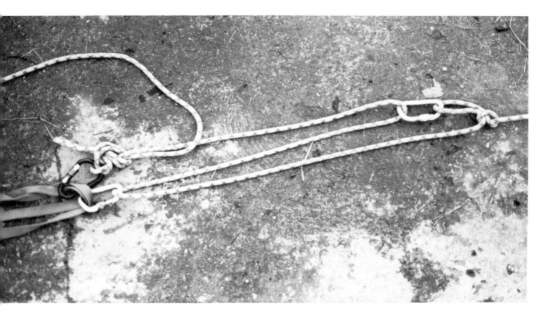

Fig 74   A way of tensioning the rope for a Tyrolean Traverse using a pulley system.

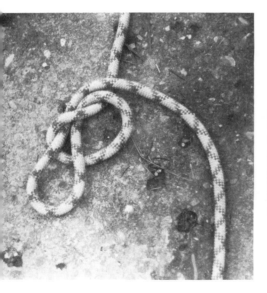

Fig 75   A loop in the main rope can be formed with a lorryman's hitch as shown here or by tying a figure of eight knot.

Fig 76   By tying the rope off with a bight as shown, the knot can be easily released if the rope needs re-tensioning. To be safe, the knot needs to be finished off with a half-hitch, passing the bight round the standing rope (as in Fig 74), so that it cannot be released accidentally.

Fig 77   The Commando Crawl – definitely not recommended in shorts!
The sling clipped to the climber's back is a safety precaution.

Fig 78   Hanging beneath the rope in a harness is the comfortable way to
do it. Here the rope has been passed through a figure-of-eight descender to
reduce friction.

4 On The Mountain

BASE CAMP

Unless you are embarking on a continuous journey through the mountains, you will need a base camp of some sort. Ideally it will have fresh running water, grass, and maybe even an overhanging boulder to use as a cooking area. Such places can often be found even among fairly recent moraines at the foot of a glacier. Unfortunately, the more comfortable the camp, the more likely it is to be accessible to marauders. Inquisitive shepherds can easily become acquisitive if they find no one at home; there have been increasing numbers of thefts in recent years, especially in South America where the distance from the nearest settlement is likely to be shorter than in the Himalaya. Of course, if you have a liaison officer and can persuade him to stay at Base Camp rather than in the nearest village, or a non-climbing friend content to stay in camp, there is no problem.

Animals can also be troublesome. Small

Fig 79   A base camp of the practical rather than idyllic kind, close to the mountain but not particularly comfortable for 'hanging out'.

mammals living among the rocks sometimes acquire a taste for expedition food. Bears have to be reckoned with in North America, and in the Arctic, polar bears can be dangerous. A rifle is a sensible weapon to carry for self-defence in some places, although it would be prohibited in others. One way of deterring bears is to surround the camp with a trip-wire running to the trigger of a rifle. It can be loaded with a blank or pointed at the sky. This method only works once, however. Probably more effective is to leave no tents standing, store or hide all food well away from other equipment, and avoid leaving behind fresh food, open tins or anything strong-smelling. The most common and destructive thieves everywhere from Alaska to the Himalaya

are ravens, and neither height nor distance are any protection from their depredations. They have extremely powerful bills and few containers will withstand their onslaught. The only safe solution is to bury food in the snow or leave it well covered with rocks. To find a much-needed cache robbed or destroyed could be disastrous.

The higher the base camp, the nearer it is to the start of the climbing and the better you will acclimatize (up to 5,500 metres, anyway), but the less relaxing it is when you return from a stint high up. In practice, the issue tends to be decided by wherever the porters, pony-men or pilot prefer to leave you. Your choice in the matter is often less than you might wish. But if you are a lightweight expedition you do have the

Fig 80   Base camp Alaska-style. Note the mound or 'shovel-up' shelter that has been dug as a food-store and kitchen.

Dhaulaghiri I from a village in the Kali Gandaki valley, Nepal

One of the hazards of Himalayan travel – local food.

Another hazard – river crossing.

Ski mountaineering in April, among the mountains of Kishtwar.

Mike Browne nearing the top of a 5,800m peak in Kishtwar.

A lightweight expedition travelling through Zanskar.

An overnight camp on a high alp in Kishtwar.

Looking towards Rakaposhi from a camp-site in the western Karakoram, near Gilgit.

Late at night off the east coast of Greenland.

Geoff Cohen and Des Rubens — a bird's eye view.

No wonder the world's glaciers are shrinking! Three days of good weather in Greenland melted away the surface of the ice to leave this tent perched on a pedestal.

Surrounded by brash ice and 'bergy-bits' heaving about on a six-foot swell, this was a bad time for the outboard to cut out . . .

Gyatso, a Zanskari pony-man.

A Thakali girl weaving, Nepal.

Strike! A liaison officer is earning his keep . . .

Carl Tobin jumars out of his tent on the East Ridge of Mount Deborah, Alaska.

Dick Isherwood at 7,000 metres on Annapurna II.

option of shifting everything further uphill if need be. You should be able to move all your gear in a couple of carries; if you can do it in a single load each, you are either very strong or you have really achieved the lightweight ideal.

RUBBISH

Fifty years ago, even twenty years ago, on all but the most prestigious or most accessible peaks, climbers were explorers treading often where no man had trod. Camped at the head of some remote valley it seemed the most natural thing in the world to tuck litter unobtrusively under a boulder. After all, no one would ever know about it. Alas, that is no longer true. The writing of this book bears witness to the explosion in expedition mountaineering, (and will, no doubt contribute to it, though I hope it will also encourage good practice). In 1986 alone, it has been estimated that 339 expeditions visited the Himalaya. Camp-sites on the Baltoro are a health hazard. Two expeditions have visited the Everest Base Camp in the last few years for the sole purpose of cleaning it up and removing rubbish. Thousands of people walk on Mount Kenya every year, and its huts are infested with rats. Hundreds more attempt one route on Mount McKinley, so that the authorities have had to instal wooden 'thrones' to cater for their needs.

We must accept that whatever we leave behind will certainly be found by others. It may seem tidily buried but, sooner or later, it will be washed out by rain, dug up by bears, discovered by ravens, or rifled by local villagers and left strewn about for the next party to discover with disgust. And where there is already litter, there is an invitation to leave more – just a little more will make no difference . . .

I have been as guilty as anyone of leaving behind fixed ropes because it seemed too dangerous to retrieve them, or caches of food because they might be useful 'another time'. Specious reasoning! Yet I am upset when I find the plastic bags and tin cans of an old camp-site, be it in Zanskar or Snowdonia. 'Do as you would be done by' – it has sometimes been called the golden rule. For our own sakes as well as for others, we must respect the mountains we enjoy so much. We can do no better than to adopt the motto of the Sierra Club:

> 'Take nothing but pictures;
> Leave nothing but footprints.'

Easy to say; not so easy to do when you are tired and run down, your shoulders are aching and you want only to get home as quickly as possible. But we *must* do it.

In practical terms, all camps need some sort of latrine, preferably a hole dug in the ground and filled in afterwards. If the surface is hard, a toilet can be constructed out of rocks. On snow, it is easy to dig a hole and line it with a plastic bag which later can be thrown down a deep crevasse. Faeces take a long time to break down at altitude; it is safer and more considerate to contain it in one spot, even if it cannot be disposed of.

Rubbish and waste food can be burned, although the foil backing of many packets cannot so you may need to rake through the ashes of the fire to retrieve it. All traces of fires should be removed, too, by scattering the ashes and replacing scorched soil. Whether non-burnable rubbish should be thrown into crevasses is controversial. It is certainly better than leaving it lying about on the surface: it is going to offend no one

Fig 81   In the third world, there is no such thing as waste disposal. The best thing is to let porters take what they want, burn what will burn and throw the rest into a deep crevasse.

and will have been crushed and ground beyond recognition by the time it emerges at the glacier snout. On the other hand, it is undeniably pollution and, taking a longer-term view of the health of this planet than our own lifetimes, we should not do it. Unfortunately, where our rubbish ends up in third-world countries when we do carry it out is an open question.

CAMPING ON SNOW

You should give much thought to where you pitch a tent on a glacier or mountain-side. Even if it is only an overnight stay, you will be spending many hours in that one place, immobile and vulnerable, so it needs to be safe. Consider what could fall from above, whether rocks, ice from a serac collapse, or powder-snow avalanches in the event of bad weather. If there is nowhere safe from these hazards, there is a strong case for digging a snow cave instead. Next, probe the whole area thoroughly. There have been many tragedies caused by climbers falling into totally unsuspected crevasses a matter of feet from their tents. An ice-axe may not be long enough to probe effectively, especially if it is a technical tool. If ski-sticks are being used, it is worth considering a pair that have been designed as an avalanche probe: the baskets are removable and the two sticks screw together. A tent pole will also do the job if the joints are taped up first.

In soft snow it pays to tread out a platform for the tent to reduce the size of the mounds and hollows that will develop beneath it. If you dig out a platform, you may be rewarded by reaching firmer snow, but you will also be providing protection from the wind.

Ordinary tent pegs are useless in soft snow. Bamboo wands can be useful for this purpose as well as for flagging a route or marking the site of a snow cave or cache. Ice-axes, shovels, skis, sticks and snow-stakes are all effective anchors for main guys, though a problem can arise if you wish to leave the tent standing and have no other anchors. In dubious weather, or in notoriously windy places like Mount McKinley, it is wise not just to put snow blocks on the valance but to build a wall right round the

*Fig 82   Spare a thought for what lies above before pitching camp.
Avalanches travel a long way. Seconds after taking this picture we were
covered in snow dust.*

Fig 83   Camping on snow is rarely comfortable.

tent. A few years ago, four of us camped on the Yanert glacier near Mount Deborah in Alaska, without taking this precaution. Within an hour of a storm blowing up, not only had all the snow been stripped from the valances, but the entire snow surface had been eroded by a foot, leaving each tent perched on a pedestal. When we felt ourselves being lifted off the ground by the wind as we lay in our sleeping bags, we realized something had to be done. More by luck than judgement we had camped beside a well-drifted moraine ridge and into this two of us dug with frantic haste while the other two held on to the tents. Eventually, we had excavated a cave large enough to take ourselves and our belongings and there,

damp but safe, we spent the rest of that wild night. A salutary experience.

It is difficult to be comfortable camping on snow. The tent fabric rustles and flaps, cold creeps up from beneath, the surface under the groundsheet quickly becomes hard and lumpy with a deep pit where you knelt unwarily on first entering the tent, and it is difficult not to bring snow inside on clothing and boots. Whenever possible, camp on rock. Even the most unpromising shelf or moraine can be made surprisingly comfortable after a few minutes work with an axe or shovel, and there will be a good chance of finding a trickle of melt-water nearby to save fuel. Sooner or later, though, camping on snow becomes inevitable. Fore-

Fig 84   If you can contrive to camp on rock it will usually be more comfortable, and certainly warmer than camping on snow.

warned is forearmed as far as the lumps go, and as for loose snow, some people favour carrying a small, stiff brush for clearing it off as they crawl into the tent.

Snow Caves

If time and snow conditions allow it, a snow cave is always preferable to a tent. It will never be quite as warm and snug as the inside of a tent when the stove is purring away; but it will usually be roomier, it can be shared by the whole team avoiding the danger of an 'us and them' mentality developing in separate tents, it will be quiet and restful whatever the weather outside and, above all, it will not blow away and leave you homeless in a hostile environment. Remember, though, that it is hard work digging a cave, especially at altitude, and will take some hours, particularly if you hit hard snow or ice. A cave can become buried by snow fall or drift, so it is important to keep a shovel inside in case you have to dig your way out, and to mark it on the outside in case you return in bad weather or after a storm. It is rare on a mountain to be able to dig a textbook snow cave. More often it is a matter of exploiting a natural feature such as a bergschrund or wind-scoop. Good sites can be found in the most unexpected places, sometimes by falling into them!

BIVOUACS

What is a bivouac? The traditional view was that it was a night out without shelter of any

Fig 85   The interior of a palatial snow cave, well lit by a candle.

Fig 86   From the point of view of energy expenditure, the best caves are found not made, like this bergschrund in which Dick Isherwood is making himself at home.

kind. Messner, on the other hand, frequently talks about bivouacs when his photographs reveal a palatial-looking hoop tent. For most people, the current definition is a night out without a tent, a tent being a structure with poles.

If you are expecting to bivouac, a sleeping bag, bivi-bag, karrimat, stove and pot are essentials. For a series of bivis some extra protection is advisable. Either you can carry a shovel and hope to dig in somewhere; or carry a zdarski sack (large bivi-sack) of gore-tex or some lighter, unproofed material, big enough for two or three people – there is plenty of scope for designing your own, as you can't usually buy them. Adding a few poles increases the weight a little but vastly increases the comfort; although, by turning a zdarski sack into a tent, you are,

strictly speaking, turning a bivouac into a camp!

If you do not intend to bivouac, the old adage applies: the more bivi gear you carry, the more likely you are to use it. Yet, at the same time, if you misjudge your strength and fitness, or the time needed for a climb, a bivouac without any gear can easily lead to frost-bite, or worse. It is impossible to generalize about what to take. It will all depend on the altitude and difficulty of the climb, the weather, your own physical and mental state and a hundred and one other variables. But there comes a time on any climb, be it a gritstone edge or Everest, when you have to go for it and rely on energy and determination. Deciding exactly when to go for it is called judgement.

On any bivi it is worth ensuring that all

Fig 87 An improbable site for a bivouac, but sometimes beggars can't be choosers.

your climbing gear and bits and pieces are gathered together in a rucksack or, if you want to use that for insulation, in a stuff sack or a large plastic bag. Especially at a comfortable bivi site in good weather it is easy to leave gear strewn around, but if it snows during the night or the wind picks up you will lose it. I like to use my boots toe to ankle with windproofs on top as a pillow, and putting them all inside the hood of my bivi bag keeps them safe. Dropping a boot on a bivouac does not bear thinking about. On steep ground, a rope slung between two anchors is useful for clipping gear on to. Strong tape loops sewn on to both inside and outside of a zdarski sack enable you to be securely belayed while inside it. Slings or rope passing through ventilation holes is asking for trouble in bad weather: snow and drift will pour in.

Fig 88   Geoff Cohen after a rough night.

COOKING

Cooking on a mountain takes far longer than normal. For a start, you need to melt snow to obtain water. In addition, food cooks less quickly at altitude because the boiling point of water is so much lower – 77°C at 7,000 metres. So-called instant foods will actually require several minutes of simmering to be reconstituted. Finally, there is the need to drink far more than normal at altitude. All these factors mean that most of your time in camp must be spent cooking, which requires both effort and fuel. Anything which will conserve fuel, like insulating the stove, putting a lid on the pot or using a wind-shield, will reduce the weight to be carried or, alternatively, increase the margin of safety in the event of bad weather high up. In general, allow one gas canister or half a litre of fuel per day for two people.

It is worth taking the trouble to cut and stack suitably-sized snow blocks at the tent entrance rather than scooping up a billy-full when needed – it's surprising how much snow is needed to cook a meal. The latter method also leaves bits of snow sticking to the outside of the pot which will melt and put out the stove if they are not removed. For the same reason, it is helpful to have some water in the bottom of the pot before you start melting snow; this reduces the condensation that will form initially on the outside of the pot, and which can also put the stove out. Digging a pit for the stove in the bell end of the tent reduces the risk of damaging, or destroying, the tent in the event of a flare-up or the tent fabric being blown inwards by wind.

It is important that the toilet area is well away from the tents and from any snow that could be used for cooking. That sounds obvious, but after a fall of snow it is easy to

Fig 89   Preparing a meal at an unusually comfortable camp-site.

use snow contaminated by yourself or, come to that, by a previous party. In heavily used areas, with limited camp sites, like the Kahiltna glacier on Mount McKinley, it is now standard practice to store all faeces in plastic bags until they can be dropped down a large crevasse.

In good weather fuel can be saved by melting snow in the sun, using a black polythene bin-liner insulated by a karrimat.

Carbon monoxide poisoning is a very real hazard when cooking in a snow cave or inside a tent. In 1986 two Swiss climbers died in their tent on McKinley in this fashion, and in Antarctica entire bases have died in their sleep. Carbon monoxide is caused by the incomplete combustion of hydro-carbons. It is given off by pressure stoves when burning with an orange rather than a blue flame, and by the solid fuel blocks used in Tommy cookers and for priming pressure stoves. It has no smell and the fumes rise to accumulate gradually in the roof. Although not actually poisonous, a build-up of carbon dioxide through inadequate ventilation, has the same effect.

I learned this lesson the hard way in the first snow cave I ever dug in the Cairngorms one January. Four of us were inside, brewing up on Hexamine blocks, in foul weather. Although we had left the entrance partly open, the cave was long and narrow and two of us were cooking at the far end of it. Suddenly my companion said 'I feel really strange' and keeled over. Alarmed, I stood up to move towards him and immediately felt my head swimming. Fortunately, the roof of the cave was thin and I was able to punch a hole through it even as I felt my knees buckling. Never has cold, fresh air felt so good.

Energy Requirements

On any mountaineering trip, your body uses up far more energy than normal, and so needs more food to supply it. Like a motor car the body needs fuel, and the harder it is working the more fuel it needs. The difference is that in cold conditions the body burns up energy simply keeping warm. Also, for every 1,000m gain in height your basal metabolic rate increases by 10 per cent, that is to say, the body becomes less efficient at converting food into energy. All these factors mean that the body's average

Fig 90 Carrying heavy loads at high altitudes uses up enormous amounts of energy which must be replaced if the body is not to deteriorate gradually.

daily requirement can increase from about 2,500 calories to nearer 6,000. Yet, at altitude, it is difficult to eat half that amount. Exhaustion, nausea, headache or sore throat can all contribute to loss of appetite, and the slowness and difficulty of melting snow in cramped conditions and the overriding need for fluids make it all too easy not to bother with food.

Napoleon realized a long time ago that an army marches on its stomach; more recently, Peter Hackett has deduced that the main cause of high altitude deterioration is shortage not of oxygen but of food. It is crucial, therefore, to have rations that are palatable, high in calories for their weight and need little or no cooking. It would be unwise to live totally on chocolate bars, however, as the energy from glucose is released rapidly and is of only short-term benefit.

Drinking

Even more important than food is drink. Shortage of food can lead to long-term deterioration, but insufficient fluid affects your performance from one day to the next and, at altitude, can be a contributory factor in pulmonary or cerebral oedema and thrombosis (*see* Chapter 5).

The human body needs about 2 litres of fluid a day at sea-level, if not exercising hard. For a mountaineer at 5,000 metres this requirement doubles to 4 litres, and at 8,000 metres it is more like 6–7 litres. Such a drastic loss of fluid is caused by sweating, heavy breathing and the diuretic effect of a hypoxic environment (which means in layman's terms that lack of oxygen makes you pee more!). Thirst is no indication of what your body actually needs. Urine colour is a better guide; the paler the better.

Fig 91   Dick Isherwood taking care of his fluid balance . . .

Much of your time and energy in camp must be spent brewing up liquid and yet more liquid. This is one reason why food tends to be overlooked, so it makes sense to have drinks with some calorific value – tea with sugar, soup, fruit drinks and hot chocolate. Coffee is less useful as caffeine is both a diuretic and makes sleep more difficult. Plain water, from snow melted in a grubby pot, is not easy to drink in sufficient quantities.

A water-bottle of at least 1 litre capacity is an essential piece of equipment. A wide mouth makes it easier to fill. A casing of closed-cell foam prevents the contents from freezing so easily. It is a good idea to keep it in your sleeping bag where it will not freeze up and is handy if you need a drink during the night. A thermos flask has advantages, especially for early starts (keeping water warm overnight), but it is heavier and easily broken.

TACTICS

There are several different ways in which the same mountain can be climbed and this needs to have been considered at the planning stage as it will influence the gear you take.

1.   Siege tactics. This approach is still remarkably popular, and not just on Everest. Numerous camps and fixed rope on anything over 30°. Slow, expensive and tedious and not even particularly safe judging by the statistics. Hardly an option for a lightweight expedition.

2.   Fix ropes for a certain distance, then pull them up, and use them again. This 'capsule-style' approach to very difficult, technical climbs was used on the West Face

of Changabang and brilliantly described by Pete Boardman in *The Shining Mountain* (Hodder and Stoughton 1978). A more recent example was the Norwegian ascent of Great Trango (see *Mountain 111*).

3.   Establish and stock a high camp or snow cave; then, when the weather is right, go for it, hoping to make it without a bivouac but not always succeeding. This is the most common approach, particularly on non-technical climbs. It is a sensible way of getting fit and acclimatized and familiar with the mountain, as well as providing something to fall back on.

4.   Start at the bottom, with no preparation, and climb straight through to the top, bivouacking or camping as many times as is necessary on the way. This is 'alpine-style'

Fig 92   Setting off on an alpine-style climb that should only take two or three days.

climbing, which has become increasingly popular over the last few years as bivi gear and footwear have improved. *Painted Mountains* by Stephen Venables (Hodder and Stoughton 1987) is an entertaining account of some recent climbs in this genre. It seems the appropriate way to climb most peaks under 6,500 metres, but is also sometimes used on much higher peaks. It was first applied to an 8,000-metre peak by Reinhold Messner and Peter Habeler when they climbed the North Face of Hidden Peak (Gasherbrum I) in 1975. Since then, some astonishingly bold and difficult climbs have been made, of which the Basque route on the South Face of Annapurna and the Schauer/Kurtyka route on the West Face of Gasherbrum IV are perhaps the most impressive.

Before trying to emulate such feats, however, it is worth pondering Pete Boardman's words written in 1973 after climbing the North Faces of Koh-i-Khaaik and Koh-i-Mondi in the Hindu Kush (the title of the article was invented by the magazine, not Pete . . .):

'The greatest advocates of ambitious alpine-style ascents of routes on high mountains in the past seem by now either to have lost their toes or their lives, or to have become wiser and more cautious. Making such ascents can be like Russian roulette with a huge revolver. You try and keep as many of its chambers as possible empty, by carefully choosing an able and speedy team and by planning the climb and the nature and weight of the food and equipment you are going to carry. However, there are three big bullets that remain – the possibility of extreme difficulty above an impossible retreat that can strand you or dangerously slow you down, the susceptibility of a small

team in the event of an accident, and the weather.'
Pete Boardman, 'Long Necks in the Hindu Kush', *Mountain 23.*

Of course, most climbers are pragmatists, adapting to circumstances whatever their intentions. An orthodox heavyweight expedition using siege tactics may, through illness and injury, end in one or two climbers making an unsupported push for the top. An early example was Hermann Buhl on Nanga Parbat in 1953, but there have been many others. At the other end of the spectrum, teams planning to climb alpine-style often find it more expedient to put in a camp or fix some rope at the bottom; and there is nothing wrong with that. In fact, awkward steps can occur anywhere, even on the walk-in, and one or two spare ropes for fixing may be found useful even by purists.
5.   Rush tactics: essentially alpine-style without equipment. Recently, the world's highest mountains have been climbed in incredibly fast times. Some of these ascents have taken advantage of other people's camps and fixed ropes; but some have been achieved quite independently in impeccable style. The ascent of Everest by Loretan and Troillet in thirty-nine hours from an advanced base camp at 5,850 metres was one such climb. Another was an ascent by Loretan, Troillet and Steiner of the East Face of Dhaulagiri in early winter (December). Leaving a snow cave at the foot of the face at midnight, they climbed for nineteen hours, spent the night out without bivi gear at the top of the face, and were still motivated enough to climb on for six hours to reach the summit; they then descended through the night back to their snow cave. In both cases the climbers carried nothing but a stove and some chocolate.

Fig 93   Technical rock-climbing at 6,000 metres. Inevitably, this sort of route will take longer than a snow climb, and sack-hauling will be necessary at times. (Note: the loop on most rucksacks is not strong enough for hauling.)

Fig 94 Technically easy climbing, but a small team at high altitude is very much out on a limb if the weather breaks.

These and other 'night-naked' ascents were recounted by Voytek Kurtyka, himself one of the most accomplished climbers in the world, in 'The Art of Suffering', *Mountain 121*. The rationale behind some, though not all, of such climbs was that by climbing at night and resting (briefly) by day it was not necessary to take extra clothing or equipment to keep warm.

Amazing though they are, in historical context these performances probably do not better the ascent of Trisul in 1907 by Tom Longstaff, the Brocherel brothers and Subadar Karbir, a Gurkha soldier. Technically a very easy climb, it was none the less the first ascent of the mountain and established a new altitude record. They climbed from a glacier camp at 5,200 metres to the summit at 7,120 metres in ten hours, and required only another three hours to descend right down to 5,000 metres. It was Longstaff who coined the descriptive phrase 'rush tactics' in *This My Voyage* (John Murray 1950). Both Longstaff's party and the Swiss had spent several weeks at around 5,000 metres, with only occasional forays higher. They were fit and thoroughly acclimatized but had suffered none of the deterioration that sets in with prolonged stays over 6,000 metres.

Potentially, this approach is extremely dangerous; and the higher the mountain the more dangerous it is. Not everybody gets away with it. Pete Thexton died of pulmonary oedema on Broad Peak having climbed from 4,910 metres to 8,000 metres in two and a half days. Greg Child's poignant account (*Mountain 94*) graphically describes the effects of high altitude on a climber's mind and body.

A KARAKORAM MIDGET

This description of an alpine-style climb on a small peak was written some years ago but conveys, I think, the flavour of a lightweight expedition.

'The camp site on the col could hardly have been bettered. The tent was pitched on a strip of shale just wide enough for it, beside a tiny turquoise tarn, twenty yards across, of clear melt water. To the west the view was obscured by an ice-wall which served as a slight shield from the prevailing wind. But to the east one looked over the green alps and wooded slopes of the Chaprot valley and down the main Hunza gorge to the northern Hispar peaks – Mohmil Sar, Trivor and Distaghil Sar. To the left of the gorge rose the 7,000 metre Pasu group and to the right, dominating all else in its proximity and symmetrical splendour, lay the massive cone of Rakaposhi. Overlooking the col to the north were the fifteen hundred feet of black, evilly loose cliffs and scree we had just descended; and above our heads was the mountain we had come to climb, rising steeply in a series of snow slopes, arêtes and rock steps to a tower which we knew to be only halfway up.

'We were not there without effort. Rob and Dave had simmered and stewed in the heat of Rawalpindi for a whole interminable fortnight before they could get a flight to Gilgit, where I was waiting with equal impatience. Once we were together, a mere two days, utilising a jeep and donkeys, had taken us as far up the Naltar valley as we wished to go. There had been the usual ailments caused by unfitness and acclimatization; but in the next four days we had transferred ourselves and our belongings from the valley floor to a 15,000ft ridge, had traversed perhaps a mile along it, and had continued over a 17,000ft peak named Snow Dome by the British party that had attempted it in 1970 – a name which seemed apt enough until we had to descend the Janus face of the mountain to reach our col.

'From the top of Snow Dome we had an excellent view of our mountain. 18,500ft high, it was a midget compared with the peaks of the Hindu Kush and Hindu Raj in the distant west, or the giants of the Karakoram stretching from Kampire Dior and the Batura group in the north-east right round to Nanga Parbat in the south-east. But for sheer beauty, in my prejudiced eyes at any rate, none of them matched our little peak. From the valley it had presented a rocky west face and an attractively steep-sided north ridge of snow broken up by some rock steps and pinnacles. But from Snow Dome it took on quite a different, almost Andean, character. The east face was revealed as a mass of deeply-etched flutings and snow-smothered rock, while our ridge twisted and curled away in a series of bewitchingly malevolent cornices. It was a beautiful sight, and a little daunting too.

'Now we were lying on warm rock in the afternoon sun, lulled by the lapping of water a few inches from the tent, gazing idly from the immensity of Rakaposhi to the distorted curves of the ridge overhead and back again, waiting for the night.

'We were away just after three. There was a waning sliver of a moon, not bright enough to dim the stars, but enough to cast my shadow on the snow. Ahead, the other two were using torches, the circles of light probing leftwards for the cornice. A breeze sent particles of snow rustling across the slope and set the laces on Rob's gaiters tap-tapping against his leg, like halyards on a mast. Occasionally there was a grunt as someone broke through the crust deep into the sugary powder beneath. Ziz-zagging up snow slopes that steepened and eased and steepened again, faithfully following the sinuations of the ridge, we gained height steadily. With the first outcrops of broken rock the climbing became more varied, scrambling up and down, traversing on snow whichever side of the ridge was easier, sometimes sliding between a rock wall and the cornice stuck on to it. As with many alpine ridges, the climbing was serious – the rock loose, the snow unstable – yet to have pitched it would have taken days, and to have moved together with the rope on would have been, in Patey's phrase, a way of dying together. (One of the problems of moving together on a corniced ridge is that, in an emergency, you have to run uphill before you can throw yourself over the other side. If this is actually accomplished, you are liable to find yourself dangling in mid-air . . .)

'The sky began to lighten, Rakaposhi took on a hazy, purplish hue and, as we abseiled down a fifty-foot wall, the sun's rays spread fan-like from behind the Pasu peaks. Briefly we were engulfed in a flood of gold. Then we were continuing up shaded snow slopes towards the halfway tower, the ridge crest to our left glittering in the sunlight.

'The tower was easier to turn than expected but having used the rope for one pitch, we moved together on a rising traverse, putting on rock runners wherever

possible. At one point a slab, three feet deep and three hundred feet wide, had broken away, exposing bare ice, but we were able to continue on snow just above the fracture and just below the cornice. The slope was becoming steeper and, crossing the runnels between rock ribs, icy. A rock buttress, the first of the real difficulties, was just ahead. Climbing straight up, on snow that became deeper and more uncertain as it steepened, I belayed at the foot of the rock and brought the others up.

'The next six hundred feet were the crux of the climb. Very little of it would have pleased a purist. Rather, it was a good old-fashioned struggle against conditions, in which the issue was always in doubt, runners few and far between, and the route really only justifiable thanks to some lucky accidents in reaching secure belays. As a rope of three it was simplest for one person to lead throughout. Dave, who had been discovering that load-carrying is not his forte, came into his own here and did a magnificent job. He coped with loose wet snow, at a ridiculous angle, with a speed and surety which Rob and I would have been hard put to match, climbed equally loose rock with the same confidence and, at the top, handled with ease a long ice-pitch which would not have disgraced a Grade IV gully. The key pitch I for one would not have cared to lead. The difficulty here was caused by a deep gully, twelve feet wide, that cut right through the mountain. It was spanned by a snow-bridge so tenuously attached at the far end that it was possible to look right through it. From this bridge it was necessary to step on to an all but vertical wall of snow overlooking the gully, roofed by icicles and, a few feet below, completely undercut. The wall had to be traversed for ten feet before a lattice-work of unsup-

Fig 95 A journey from Gilgit first by jeep . . .

needed wringing out periodically. Now the sun was sinking. Rob was muttering about bivouac sites but Dave and I preferred not to hear. Over two rock bumps, then an unwelcome hundred-foot drop and an exposed climb out of the gap on precarious snow, which we should have pitched but, in our urgency, didn't. More bumps, more ridge, and glimpses of huge cornices visible only when passed. At last nothing but a few hundred feet of snow slope, with some crevasses to side-step. Dave was tired – not surprisingly – and Rob was feeling the altitude. I took over the lead, glad of an opportunity to contribute something, even if it was just trampling a trail through deep snow.

Fig 96   . . . and then with donkeys, took us as far up the valley as we wished to go.

ported ice served as a bridge for the last few feet to solid rock. How the whole thing held I just don't know. Even following was an unnerving experience. I was careful to put prussiks on the rope for if any of that fragile structure had given way, having first hit the gully wall, one would have been left hanging with little or no chance of climbing out. Dave, however, simply took it in his stride in a remarkable display of sang-froid.

'The technical difficulties were confined to those six hundred feet, but the climb was far from over. Time had been passing all too rapidly. Although huge cumulo-nimbus clouds had obscured Rakaposhi and the Batura group and the occasional outrider had drifted in our direction, the sun had been beating down most of the day. Breeches had long been saturated by soggy snow and melting ice, and mittens had

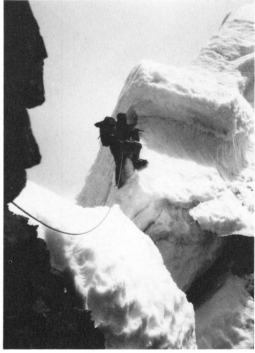

Fig 97   Dave Wilkinson tackling the crux pitch on Mehrbani.

Fig 98 *Rob Ferguson moving on to pastures new after the ascent of Mehrbani.*

'The summit was a snow ridge, slightly corniced. We chopped it down and sat on the crest in a row. I don't think any of us felt particularly excited – just tired, and aware that both night and a storm were creeping up menacingly. The thunder clouds had become a grey pall which, while we were not looking, had crept past us and spread west, obscuring the sun. As we watched, the pall began to drop and move towards us, obliterating peaks as it came. The sun re-appeared for a few brief moments as we descended, gilding the snows in eerie contrast to the darkness of the sky. Then it disappeared and the greyness was all about us.

'There was a hold-up in the descent. At the back, I could not see what was causing it for a hump in the ridge. Standing on the crest holding coils, I waited impatiently. A few beads of hail fell and the surface of the snow seemed to be spluttering. Suddenly my hair felt strange. Putting up a hand, I found it was rising of its own accord. When my axe began to hum as well, I dived for the nearest boulder – partly to avoid being the most prominent object on the ridge but chiefly, I must confess, from an irrational desire to be out of sight of whoever sits up there throwing thunderbolts.

'However, we were lucky. By the time we had dug out a comfortable bivouac platform and settled into our bags, the hail had stopped and there were even a few stars. There were one or two showers in the night, but by morning the weather was as good as ever, the big peaks having borne the brunt of the storm.

'Four full-length abseils took us down the difficulties next day. After a short traverse we climbed straight down steep snow, which defied all the laws by turning to ice at the bottom, on to a small hanging glacier. This enabled us to bypass much of the ridge, regaining it just before the initial snow slopes. From this point one could look down nearly a thousand feet on to the brilliant splash of blue on the col and the welcoming yellow speck of the tent beside it. At the sight, the elation which had been so conspicuously absent on the summit welled up. Mingling with pleasure in the magnificence of our surroundings and delight at the isolation of our position, it became a conscious, exuberant happiness as I hurried on down. Being conscious, it was accompanied by gratitude – to Rob and Dave, to the weather, not least to the mountain itself. We decided to call it Mehrbani which, besides being suitably euphonious, in Urdu means "thank you".

'That was only the beginning. In the next fortnight we crossed two passes, one of them a new one, travelled four little-known glaciers, made the first ascent of an easy peak of 19,500ft and, right at the end, tightening our belts, were only foiled in a rapid dash up a peak of 22,500ft by bad weather. It was a marvellous, if strenuous, taste of mountain exploration in which the available maps were often no more than misleading outlines, and every new viewpoint seemed to yield a fresh surprise and another puzzle.

'Back in Gilgit we did some sums. Leaving aside air travel to and from Pakistan, our "expedition" had cost £30 a head.'

Climber and Rambler, June 1976

117

5   Medical Problems

A few years ago four of us flew into Lhasa airport, in Tibet. Lhasa is situated on a high plateau at 3,600 metres above sea level. On the long drive from the airport to the town we were held up at some roadworks. Glad of an excuse to stretch my legs after five days of sitting in aeroplanes, I strolled up the line of waiting vehicles to see what the problem was. There was nothing to see so I carried on walking. Suddenly there was a shout and I saw several men racing for cover in a culvert under the road. Some not-so-subtle instinct told me I should do the same and I covered those fifty yards in a time that Ben Johnson would have been proud of. As I dived beneath the road to join the grinning Tibetan workmen there was an explosion followed by a shower of earth, stones and sizeable boulders. Then I became aware of the altitude. My chest felt tight and I was gasping and heaving for breath. I spent the rest of the day with a splitting headache ...

ACCLIMATIZATION

Medically speaking, anything over 2,400 metres is a high altitude, although the specific problems associated with altitude, such as acute mountain sickness and pulmonary and cerebral oedema, usually occur above 3,500 metres. They are a direct result of hypoxia, or oxygen starvation. The proportion of oxygen in the atmosphere, about 20 per cent, is much the same on the summit of Everest as it is at sea-level; but the decrease in atmospheric pressure with altitude means that there are fewer oxygen molecules to a given volume of air and that the pressure needed to push oxygen from the air sacs (alveoli) of the lung into the blood vessels surrounding them is reduced. The result is that at 5,500 metres there is only half the oxygen available for the body that there is at sea-level, and on top of Everest only one-third.

Everest is actually in an area of high atmospheric pressure compared to the sub-arctic regions, thanks to the circulation of warm and cold air masses high up. This explains why Mount McKinley in Alaska 'feels' higher than 6,194 metres; Doug Scott compared it to a 7,000-metre peak in the Himalaya. Pressure is also subject to seasonal variations, becoming generally lower in winter. According to Michael Ward this is as significant a factor as low temperatures and high winds in winter ascents of very high mountains. ('The Mountaineer at Extreme Altitude', *Alpine Journal 1888–89*. *See also* John B. West, 'Oxygenless Climbs and Barometric Pressure', *American Alpine Journal 1984*.)

Up to a height of around 5,500 metres the body can adjust to lack of oxygen by numerous little adaptations which are not totally understood. It is believed that 80 per cent of acclimatization is complete within ten days, and 95 per cent within six weeks. This does not mean that the body can function exactly as it would at sea-level: any sort of hard work will result in panting and one simply cannot walk uphill at anything like a normal pace. But it does mean that there are no harmful effects from living at that altitude. Above 5,500 metres, or there-

Fig 99   Geoff Cohen feeling the altitude at 6,000 metres.

*Fig 100   Plenty of time should be allowed
for acclimatization before setting off on any
serious climb.*

Ideally, a week should be allowed, with rest
days on the way, before sleeping at 5,000
metres. Problems occur when people are in
a hurry, either because they are fit and full
of energy, or because they have a tight time
schedule. The route to Everest Base Camp is
notorious. Trekkers fly to Lukla at 2,825
metres and try to walk up to the Base Camp
at 5,300 metres without allowing their
bodies time to adjust. The results are often
fatal. Mount Kenya is another area that sees
a lot of high altitude casualties every year,
because of its accessibility. It is possible to
be on top of Point Lenana (4,985 metres) not
much more than forty-eight hours after
leaving London. I know, because I have
done it in a 'controlled' medical experiment,
but I certainly would *not* recommend it. For
climbers going above 7,000 metres, the ideal
seems to be a long period of acclimatization
at around 5,000 metres, with occasional trips
higher, followed by a rapid push on the
actual climb.

ACUTE MOUNTAIN SICKNESS

AMS is a common consequence of ascending
too far, too fast, although some people will
suffer however careful they are. It is as
common on Mont Blanc as it is in the
Himalaya. The term 'acute' does not refer
to the severity of the symptoms, but is used
in its medical sense of 'appearing after or
persisting for a relatively brief period of
time' (as opposed to 'sub-acute' and 'chronic'
mountain sickness in which acclimatization
does not take place at all). AMS is unpleasant
but not in itself a dangerous condition. It
needs to be taken seriously, however, as it
makes clear thinking difficult and can
develop into pulmonary or cerebral oedema.

abouts, the body ceases to acclimatize any
further and gradual deterioration sets in.
Above 7,000 metres the process accelerates,
although dehydration and lack of food also
play a major part. The adage 'climb high,
sleep low' relates both to this and to the fact
that hypoxia is increased at night when the
rate and depth of breathing are reduced
during sleep.

The key to successful acclimatization is a
very slow rate of ascent, far slower than
seems necessary at the time, preferably
carrying a light pack and not working hard.

Symptoms do not occur immediately but after twelve hours or more and usually subside within a day or two. Typical symptoms are headache, dizziness, loss of appetite, nausea, tiredness and yawning. They tend to become worse at night when the rate and depth of breathing are reduced; sleeping tablets do not help as they depress respiration further, so that even less oxygen is available. If you are suffering from AMS do not attempt to go any higher. Normally, a couple of paracetamol tablets and a day's rest will put you right. If the symptoms persist for more than two days, or become worse rather than better, go down to a lower altitude.

A common feature of AMS, especially at night, is Cheyne-Stokes breathing. The cycle begins with a few shallow breaths which become deeper and longer and then suddenly stop altogether. I first learned about it lying in a tent with two others at 5,000 metres. When I heard the breathing stop I thought for a horrible moment that someone had died and I had time to wonder whether it was my wife or my best friend before the breathing started again. It was only after the cycle had been repeated several times that I realized I was listening to myself.

Peripheral oedema, a swelling of hands, feet or face, sometimes occurs but it is not dangerous or significant and subsides gradually of its own accord.

Diamox

Diamox (acetazolamide) is a drug which has become widely used over the last few years to prevent, or reduce, the symptoms of AMS. Recently, it has been suggested that it can also be used as a treatment for AMS, and experiments have shown that it increases the oxygen in the blood by 20 per cent at altitudes up to 5,600 metres, thus improving acclimatization. It is now being used as an aid to performance at much higher altitudes: 'Anecdotal reports indicate its usefulness at up to 7,000 metres on Everest and there is no reason to suggest it will not work even higher' (quoted from *The Use of Acetazolamide at Altitude*, a paper produced by the Birmingham Medical Research Expeditionary Society).

How it works is not completely understood. It was first used as a diuretic, to reduce fluid retention in the body and thus reduce susceptibility to pulmonary and cerebral oedema. It is now believed that its most beneficial effect is to increase the rate and depth of breathing, especially important at night when these rates would normally drop.

A common side-effect is tingling in the fingers, feet and face, but it can also cause vomiting, dizziness and drowsiness and, very occasionally, more serious problems. Dr Charles Clarke suggests taking it twice a day for two days before leaving home to see how you react to it. If all goes well, he advocates taking it twice a day for three days before going to altitude and continuing up to 5,000 metres. It is only available on prescription, however, so you will have to consult your own doctor about this.

If Diamox really does improve performance high on a mountain (which is not yet proven), as well as preventing AMS lower down, climbers have an ethical decision to make. It is complicated by the fact that more oxygen in the blood will not only make them stronger but will also enable them to think more clearly, bringing safety as well as achievement into the equation. It may be a difficult temptation to resist. Your choice...

Pulmonary and Cerebral Oedema

These are two extremely serious forms of AMS caused by fluid collecting in the lungs and in the brain respectively. Both develop very quickly. In the former, as the alveoli of the lungs become filled with fluid rather than air, less and less oxygen is absorbed into the blood until the nervous system is affected and breathing stops. Many of the symptoms are the same as AMS but in addition the patient feels breathless even when resting, and a persistent cough develops, producing a frothy phlegm which may become blood-streaked. Sometimes bubbling sounds can be heard in the chest. Confusion and irrational behaviour occur, and finally unconsciousness. Death follows within a few hours.

In the less common cerebral oedema the main symptoms are severe headache and a loss of balance and coordination, so that the sufferer stumbles and staggers or has difficulty using a mug or a spoon.

Both these conditions are most common among trekkers at heights of 3,500–5,000 metres, but they do affect well-acclimatized mountaineers at higher altitudes. Who is affected, and when, seems to be unpredictable. Marcel Ruedi, for instance, died while descending Makalu, his tenth 8,000-metre peak. Chris Chandler's sudden collapse on Kangchenjunga is another harrowing example (Cherie Bremer-Kamp, *Living on the Edge*, David and Charles 1987); but there have been all too many others. What is certain, however, is that a respiratory infection is a predisposing factor in pulmonary oedema; to go high with a cold or a cough is asking for trouble.

The only real remedy is oxygen, either bottled if it is available, or, preferably, rapid descent. If the terrain permits, it is worth descending even in the dark; by morning it may be too late. Dexamethasone is a steroid that has recently been used successfully in the treatment of AMS and pulmonary and cerebral oedema. Lasix (frusemide), a diuretic, has been a recommended treatment for some years. Opinion now is divided over its usefulness, but it will be easier for the unqualified to obtain and travel with than a steriod, and is certainly worth trying in an emergency. Neither of these drugs should be used prophylactically.

THROMBOSES

At altitude the blood thickens because more red oxygen-carrying blood corpuscles are being produced. Dehydration reduces the blood volume, making it even thicker, and both stress and hypoxia make it more liable to form clots. Over 7,000 metres, clotting of the blood becomes a distinct possibility, especially after a long period of immobility in a storm. A clot forming in a leg (deep vein thrombosis) causes swelling and pain, but if it becomes detached from the wall of the vein, it can be carried upwards to lodge in a lung as a pulmonary embolus. This is characterized by pain in the chest and difficulty in breathing and is very serious.

A blood clot forming in the brain (cerebral thrombosis) causes a stroke which can cause temporary or permanent paralysis, usually to one side of the body. On the disastrous Makalu expedition of 1961 Ed Hillary had a stroke at 5,800 metres and Peter Mulgrew collapsed with a pulmonary embolus at 8,200 metres (Michael Ward, *In This Short Span*, Gollancz 1972). There have been several more recent examples. Climbing at very high altitudes is hazardous.

FROSTBITE

Frostbite is a freezing of the tissues which occurs at cold temperatures and can result in permanent damage and even loss of limbs. In mountaineering it is almost never caused by cold alone, but by cold in combination with one or more of the following factors:

1.   Wind – which not only affects exposed flesh (the 'wind-chill factor') but decreases the overall body temperature by violently moving the air trapped within clothing. Windproof overmitts are important in extreme conditions, as are finger gloves for doing fiddly jobs, and wrist-loops on mittens to avoid losing them.
2.   Dehydration – lack of fluid results in a reduction in blood volume and a withdrawal of blood from the extremities to ensure a supply to the brain and other vital organs. Without a good supply of warm blood, the tissues are far more likely to freeze.
3.   Hypothermia – which often goes hand in hand with frostbite. Cold, exhaustion and lack of food lead to a lowering of the body's core temperature, a reduction in blood volume and a withdrawal of blood from the extremities.
4.   Constriction of the circulation – this is especially liable to occur with the feet. A second pair of socks can have the opposite of the intended effect. If you buy a pair of alveolite inner boots you will need a larger size of plastic shells to accommodate them; your normal shells will cause constriction.

Being furthest from the heart and the first affected by a reduced supply of blood, hands and feet are the most vulnerable parts of the body. Nose and cheeks, although exposed to the air, are also the most easily detected and re-warmed, especially if people keep an eye

on each other. There are usually no symptoms unless one counts numbness and loss of sensation which easily go unnoticed in big boots. The skin becomes yellow-white and hard to the touch.

Superficial frostbite (frost-nip) can be reversed quickly by putting a hand over nose, cheek or ear, fingers inside your clothing, and feet inside someone else's clothing; but the affected area will need to be looked after, as it is likely to freeze again. In the case of a foot or toes that are badly frostbitten and do not soon revive, it may be better to leave them frozen during the descent, as more damage can be caused by climbing or walking on them once they have thawed out. Once back at base, or if you are stuck at a high camp, it is best to re-warm the frozen parts rapidly (in hot water that is just bearable to the fingers), until the tissues become soft. More hot water will be needed from time to time to keep the temperature constant. During and after re-warming the injury will be extremely painful warranting strong painkillers.

Once the part has thawed out, a blister or blisters usually form. If they are filled with clear fluid, the prognosis is good; bloody and discoloured fluid is less hopeful. Either way, it is crucial that the blisters should not be broken as infection then becomes all but inevitable. They should be wrapped in cotton wool, keeping fingers and toes separate, and lightly bandaged, every precaution being taken to avoid direct pressure or rubbing. The dressing should be changed daily and the injury bathed in warm sterile water. Smoking should be avoided at this stage as nicotine is a vasco-constrictor, reducing the blood supply to the extremities. Alcohol has the opposite effect, so can be helpful in a warm, controlled situation. If the blisters *are* broken (as they will be if the patient has to walk on them) a course of antibiotics should be started as soon as possible.

After several days the blisters subside and, after an alarming multi-coloured phase, a black scab forms beneath which regeneration often takes place. Eventually this sloughs off or, in severe cases, whole digits may come away. Amputation is usually only resorted to if the limb becomes badly infected or to 'tidy up' after the dead tissue has fallen off.

In the past climbers have taken Ronicol pills to increase the flow of blood to the extremities. Present thinking, however, regards this as unlikely to be effective in preventing frostbite.

6 'Small Expeditions in the Himalaya'

This article was written for the 1979 *Alpine Journal*. It was deliberately provocative, but there is little in it I wish to alter. Nor has all that much changed, apart from the number of expeditions involved. Trevor Braham, whose book *Himalayan Odyssey* (Allen and Unwin 1974) is a fascinating account of a lifetime of lightweight exploration and mountaineering, estimates in the 1988–89 *Alpine Journal* that there were no less than 339 climbing expeditions in the Greater Himalaya in 1986, of which two-thirds were large ones.

'Ever since climbers first began to visit the Himalaya at the end of the last century there have been large expeditions and small ones. Mummery, invited to join Conway's lavish investigation of the Karakoram, preferred to go to Nanga Parbat with Hastings and Collie and a couple of Gurkhas. While the Workmans and the Duke of the Abruzzi were invading the Karakoram with their miniature armies, Dr A. M. Kellas was making some remarkable journeys of exploration in Sikkim and climbing peaks up to 7,000m with only a few local porters for company. Between the wars there was a sharp contrast between the series of heavyweight expeditions to Everest, Kangchenjunga and Nanga Parbat, and the explorations of Shipton and Tilman or the success of Spencer Chapman on Chomolhari. During the so-called golden age of the fifties and early sixties when the majority of big Himalayan peaks were being climbed, most expeditions were large, for nationalism, denounced by the Alpine Club in the thirties, was more blatantly and internationally rife than ever it had been on the Eigerwand and Grandes Jorasses. But there were notable exceptions – the Austrians on Cho Oyu and Broad Peak, the British on the Muztagh Tower and the American four-man attempt on Everest. The last fifteen years have seen Everest firmly established as an international status symbol, permanently booked up five years in advance. Not only Everest but all Nepal's 8,000m peaks have been repeated time and time again, confounding Longstaff's hope that once Everest had been climbed mountaineers would forget about mere height and "turn to the true enjoyment of the Himalayas, most likely to be found at 20,000ft or less". More recently, the re-opening of the Karakoram by Pakistan has sent a fresh series of massive caravans winding up the Baltoro. At the other end of the scale, there have been the groups of two, three or four climbers posing as tourists in an effort to evade increasing restrictions, regulations and expense, unobtrusively penetrating the remotest corners of the Himalaya and making many fine first ascents among the lower peaks. Initially most of these small expeditions were Austrian or Japanese, but numbers of British climbers have begun to follow suit. This trend must have been strengthened by articles by Dennis Gray, Trevor Braham and Joe Tasker which have appeared in the *Alpine Journal* over the last few years, arguing basically that large expeditions are anachronistic. Dennis Gray in 1971 was describing the "approach and style of application" of the first ascents of Annapurna and Everest as being "as relative to this day as the stage coach to jet travel". He went on to comment that "to the discerning, success means nothing, only the way it has been achieved matters". In Britain, at any rate, a climate of opinion seems to have been created in which small expeditions are regarded as desirable, whether it be from the standpoint of personal satisfaction, the health of climbing as a sport or the ecology of the Himalaya. And yet large expeditions remain the norm in Himalayan climbing.

Cast an eye down the long list of expeditions that every year visit the Karakoram and Nepal and you will find that the vast majority have at least 8 members, supported by Sherpas or high-altitude porters, employ over 100 porters to reach their Base Camp and cost many thousands of pounds. Clearly, whatever the pundits say about small expeditions, climbers internationally are not convinced. Why should this be so?

'I have to plead ignorance of the mechanics of organising a large expedition and hope I will be forgiven if I am simplifying, but there seem to be certain discernible strands of logic influencing the initial conception. One is the need for publicity as an aid to

Fig 101   In the days before air travel became relatively cheap, the overland route to the Himalaya was a popular alternative, with the added advantage of being able to take quantities of pre-packed food. This journey is still possible, avoiding Afghanistan by travelling through southern Iran.

raising funds. Despite the startling achievements of Reinhold Messner, it is still highly unlikely that the media would give the same publicity, before the event at any rate, to a small expedition as it would to a large one, whatever its objective, so organisers tend to think in grandiose terms from the start.

'A side-effect of publicity is the survival of nationalism in mountaineering, a fact to which the Nepalese Rules for Expeditions bear witness. The rules stipulate that the Liaison Officer should be equipped with a Nepalese flag to be planted on the summit alongside the national flag of the expedition. The officials of the Ministry of Tourism were genuinely puzzled that we should neither have nor want a flag of our own. "But *all* expeditions have a flag", one of them remarked plaintively. Few expeditions nowadays are totally financed and organised on a national basis. But the requirements of the media are such that any expedition with a sufficiently formidable objective – and this can mean high rather than hard – and, above all, big enough to gain credibility, will soon become a national event, "invested", as Shipton complained years ago, "with a glamour foreign to the fundamental simplicity of the game". Climbers become national figures and under strong pressure to succeed, if only because they know they have an audience; and success is interpreted in the same distasteful manner as an Olympic gold medal.

'The principle that size inspires confidence is as true in the attracting of financial sponsors as it is in the apparently necessary preliminaries of winning over the media. The team must be large, equipment the best, the budget enormous, or the men of business will not be impressed. Heavy commitment to a particular sponsor, or a film or book contract dependent on success, can exert a pressure similar to that of national expectations. And should there have been little publicity beforehand, the sponsor or sponsors will soon rectify the situation.

'But whether it is financial obligation, an armchair audience or personal ambition of a not strictly mountaineering nature that is the original motivating force behind the size of a big expedition or, most likely, a blend of all three, success becomes all important and no expense is spared to ensure it. Lavish plans become yet more lavish. To eliminate the possibility of human weakness and to enable the climbers to conserve their energy for the summit, Sherpas are employed to do the hard, and often the most dangerous, work (ferrying loads through the Khumbu ice-fall into the Western Cwm, for instance). All these people, both climbers and Sherpas, have to be fed, clothed and tented, and maybe supplied with oxygen as well to make assurance doubly sure, which means the endless carrying of a vast amount of food and equipment up the mountain – most of it catering for the carriers. Ropes must be fixed to make this process easier and safer and camps must be close together for the Sherpas to get there and back in a day. (Many modern Sherpas – and this is a reflection not on them but on their employers – are much more at home with a pair of jumars than with an ice-axe.) Finally, each camp must be connected by radio so that the whole gigantic operation can be efficiently directed from below (and, on the recent French expedition to Everest, so that the climbers could speak to their wives in Paris). All this costs an awful lot of money. The only element in success which cannot be bought is the weather and this, alas, is often the decisive one.

'On some expeditions of this type an unconscious belief that there is safety in numbers seems to lull climbers into a false sense of security which influences their assessment of objective dangers. This could be one reason for the frighteningly high accident rate on the big peaks. Certainly, that sense of physical isolation, commitment, self-reliance, call it what you will, which is at once so disturbing and so exhilarating and which, if pressed, I would say is what mountaineering is all about, must be virtually nil until the summit bid. In this context, it is interesting to note Chris Bonington's comments on the climbing of Brammah I (6,400m) in Kishtwar with Nick Estcourt: "It had been a mountain holiday rather than an expedition and yet the climbing, without fixed rope and with a long summit push had, in some ways, been more committing than what we had experienced on Everest the previous autumn."

'The preconceptions, then, of journalists and captains of industry go a long way towards preserving that elephantine anachronism, the large expedition, and their support, once elicited, is interpreted in terms of more men, more equipment, more money. Another factor tending to make expeditions bigger than they need be is the expense involved in gaining permission to climb. To a large expedition, the money involved is a bagatelle, but to an otherwise modest venture it can be crippling. In Nepal, for instance, you pay a peak fee of £500. Then you must fully equip a liaison officer. He will not go above Base Camp (in fact, of the three LOs with whom I have had dealings, a Pakistani, an Indian and a Nepali, not one has even got that far), but he must be equipped as well as the climbers and everything must be new. There are plenty of Sherpas in Kathmandu to tell him if he has not been given the very best – "Aha! Only a Redline. We had those in the Ice-fall" – and

they will probably buy the gear off him afterwards. To add insult to injury, he must be paid over and above his police salary (and at a higher rate), and insured. For the average Nepali sub-inspector it is like a cricketer or footballer being given a benefit match, and he is determined to make the most of it. Moreover, the LO cannot be left on his own at Base Camp, if he reaches it, so the expedition must employ a cook who also must be paid, equipped and insured. And because the LO's main function is to send weekly reports to the Tourist Ministry, there has to be a mail runner as well. By the time these extra mouths have been fed and extra porters hired to carry their food and belongings, the expedition has been compelled to spend nearly £1,500 for its peak and the doubtful benefit of an LO to organise its transport and porters. For a small expedition this could well be over half its total budget. The situation is very similar in Pakistan, though not yet so bad in India where the peak fee is lower and the LO is expected to return his gear. For a small expedition the temptation *not* to seek official permission can be well-nigh irresistible. One alternative is simply to increase the number of climbers so as to share the expense, on the assumption that they already own the necessary equipment; but many organisers are tempted into the vicious circle of publicity, sponsorship and even greater expense to ensure success.

'A final factor making for large expeditions is lack of confidence. There are three essential attributes for a Himalayan climber: alpine experience, a strong stomach and the ability to acclimatize. The last is difficult to predict – many a fine climber has failed in the Himalaya on this count – though how you feel on top of Mont Blanc, is, in most cases, a fair indication of how you will react higher up. The need for a strong stomach is not so bizarre as it may seem. Our excessively hygienic attitude towards food in the West leaves many of us unduly susceptible to any different forms of bacteria, not necessarily virulent ones. Yet to avoid all local food and drink is to take a lot of meaning out of the journey to and from the mountain which, for all but the most myopic, is as important a part of an expedition as the climb. General Bruce wrote, "One point to which I must again draw attention, and which is the most important of all for the explorer of the Himalaya and especially for the mountaineer – that is to have a really dependable digestion . . ." Finally, experience of alpine or other glaciated mountains is of far more value than great technical skill, which will rarely be needed. Anyone who has the physical fitness and the mental approach – in particular the refusal to be intimidated by appearances or scale (which is not the same as ignoring objective dangers) – to climb a *grande course* can attempt a Himalayan peak with a reasonable chance of success. But the Himalaya are now so accessible and have been described and photographed so alluringly that, not unnaturally, many people wish to climb there who do not possess these attributes. Lacking confidence in their own ability, or perhaps worried by the hazards of

Fig 102   The walk-in can be enjoyable and interesting, and is a chance to get fit and acclimatize. As well as being more pleasant, it is easier for the body to acclimatize if a big pack is not carried.

illness and altitude, they take refuge in numbers and the support (sometimes, indeed, the leadership) of Sherpas.

'And so the large expedition still exists and, in all probability, will continue to do so. Like Concorde, it will remain of immense importance to those involved, arousing admiration in the ignorant and indignation in the concerned. To me, it seems that the amount of money spent on the largest expeditions – £100,000 is not an unusually high figure – is shameful and quite unjustifiable. To argue that it is but a fraction of a big company's advertising budget or that far more is spent on football is beside the point when such a sum is not necessary to climb a mountain, however high or difficult.

'Returning to small expeditions, confusion reigns over what exactly the term means. Nowadays nearly every expedition from Britain pays lip-service to the ideal – even the recent K2 expedition was described as "small", which, relative to other K2 expeditions, it may have been – yet some are clearly smaller than others. And is size gauged by numbers or expense, or both? It is possible for a six-man expedition to cost half as much as a two-man expedition with a more ambitious objective or more extravagant notions.

'I wish to put forward a definition of a small expedition as one in which all equipment and food can be carried on its members' backs in a single load. Indeed, a provocative demon urges me to go further, to put my head on the block, and declare that *all* Himalayan expeditions should conform to this criterion. Such an approach to big mountains would mean that certain problems would have to wait until there were men and materials capable of overcoming them. But is that any different from

saying that a rock-climb should be left for the man able to climb it free?

'I would not insist that the expedition carry everything itself on the approach march, only that it should be able to do so if, for instance, the porters went on strike. Few of us from cold climates can cope at once with the fierce heat of the foothills, and it is difficult to appreciate the flora, fauna and culture of the country through which you pass with a huge load on your back. It could be argued that, by the same token, it is not possible to enjoy climbing a mountain with a load on your back and it is, therefore, only sensible to employ Sherpas to do it. I would reply that climbing – of any sort – is only partly to do with conscious pleasure and enjoyment and much more to do with those fleeting but highly-prized moments which, for the sake of argument, I shall call happiness:

> "The moment of happiness – not the sense of well-being,
> Fruition, fulfilment, security or affection,
> Or even a very good dinner, but the sudden illumination . . ."

'Probably few of us have experienced quite the sort of revelation Eliot is talking about, but many would agree that on a climb where mind and muscle are being, or have just been, taxed to the utmost, what they feel goes far beyond enjoyment, even if it is difficult to put into words and never lasts for long.

'In the valleys the expedition can live off the land, saving its own food for higher up. This in itself will limit the number of climbers, for few Himalayan villages have the resources to feed large groups. Once the last village is left behind, the porters must be paid off, for now the expedition is living off its own fat (literally, no doubt, as well as metaphorically) and it will have to move faster than most porters are prepared to do. I have found it feasible to pack everything needed for three weeks in the mountains, with alpine-style mixed climbing in mind, into a 75lb load. This is most easily done with a party of three crammed into a lightweight two-man tent, as the cooking and climbing gear is no greater than it would be for two. There are plenty of other ways of saving weight. If I know it is all going on my own back, I personally carry no spare clothing except a pair of socks, and I am not convinced that a duvet jacket is necessary below 8,000m. Several pounds can be saved by eschewing reflex cameras and additional lenses, and transistor radios, cassette tape recorders and the other means by which we insulate ourselves from our surroundings, are out of the question. Fuel can be saved by relying more on wood and dried dung, always available up to 3,650m and often much higher, than on gaz or paraffin. It is worth remembering Tilman's advice that "on any expedition, even the most serious, the tendency to take two of everything, just to be on the safe side, needs to be firmly suppressed". Tilman's words were endorsed by Lionel Terray, writing of the Alps just after the war when "both food and equipment were very much heavier than they are now, but above all we were weighed down by traditions as old as mountaineering itself. People always carried a little more food and gear than they really needed, just in case". With the carefully designed pack-frames now on the market, it ought to be possible for climbers of average physique but sufficient determination to carry loads of 90lb or more up to, say, 4,000m. With greater care in the selection of

Fig 103   Climbing alpine-style at 6,000 metres in the Himalaya.

food and equipment and a more drastic pruning of luxuries, it might well be possible for an expedition to be self-contained for five or six weeks. Admittedly, this would still impose severe restrictions on the ascent of a peak like K2 at the far end of the Baltoro galcier. But the effort would be worth making even there, for the right people; and for lesser mortals (myself definitely included!) there are plenty of easier and more accessible peaks in the Himalaya.

'Load-carrying is enjoyable only in a masochistic sense (though it often *is* enjoyable in that sense, believe it or not) but as with so many things, the reward is in proportion to the effort expended. For anyone who loves mountains and hates crowds, the satisfaction of travelling through wild, empty glaciated country, pitching a

Fig 104   Climbing on a rock peak in the Kulu district of India.

solitary tent every night in a new place and, perhaps as the climax but not the end of the journey, reaching a summit, must surely be self-evident. Had Shipton and Tilman been able to exchange their Meade tents, Bergen rucksacks and sacks of flour and rice for the lightweight food and equipment now available, that is how they would have been climbing. "The unattainable ideal to be kept in mind", wrote Tilman of the 1938 Everest expedition, "is two or three men carrying their food with them as in the Alps." The unattainable is now, I believe, attainable. I know it to be a perfectly feasible approach to small peaks up to 6,500m and I can see no valid reason why it should not be applied to almost any peak; though I would echo Bruce's remark that "the true enjoyment of the Himalaya . . . is to be found in the lesser ranges". It is also a very cheap way of

climbing. By turning a blind eye to officialdom, it is still possible to organize a three-man trip to the Himalaya for £1,000, including air travel.

'Granted, with less time at your disposal you are at the mercy of the weather and the chances of failure are high; but on the other hand, if you are not establishing camps and fixing ropes, a short spell of good weather will suffice to climb most peaks, as Messner has demonstrated several times. Without the compelling need to succeed that bedevils the large expedition, many climbers will admit defeat more easily than they would be allowed to if they were part of a team; but if survival is regarded as more important than success, this is not necessarily a bad thing.

'And if you do fail, what of it? The personal rewards will have been great even if public acclaim is lacking. Mountaineering

Fig 105   A small expedition on the approach to Brammah II, a fine peak
in Kishtwar.

is, after all, a sport, not a war, however much the language of the press may try to persuade us otherwise. Because the World Cup and the Olympic Games display so many of the characteristics of war, perhaps that is all the more reason for mountaineers to avoid a similar confusion of ends and means. In the literature of the world, mountains have traditionally been sources of inspiration, symbols of aspiration to a better life and a refuge from the values of the market-place. The early mountaineers seem to have been aware that they inherited this tradition and trod softly over the mountains they loved. Today, not only businessmen in search of a quick profit but climbers like ourselves are trampling on them, dragging the market-place lock, stock and barrel into the hills, even into the Himalaya, right up to the summit of Everest.'

7 Afterwards

One of the delightful things about a lightweight expedition is that once you are back home you can enjoy living with your memories, but there is little else to be done. If you have received an MEF grant you will have to write a brief account, but that is all. There is no need for an expensive, glossy-covered, illustrated report that will keep you busy for months.

If you have taken colour slides on the trip and decide to show them to an audience, be it your family, the local WI or the Alpine Club, it pays to be selective. Show only your best pictures and adapt the narrative to fit the slides, rather than feeling you must illustrate the whole expedition from start to finish. On the whole, pictures with people in them are more interesting than landscapes. Close-ups always go down well. Badly exposed or out-of-focus slides may have significance for you but they will only lead to yawns. 'Star-bursts' are dramatic but only work once. Unless you are a spell-binding raconteur or the most gifted of photographers, an hour is the longest you can expect to hold anyone's attention, however devoted to you or interested in the topic. Aim to show a hundred slides at most, in forty-five minutes, and you can't go far wrong.

WHAT NEXT?

If you enjoy your lightweight expedition as much as I have enjoyed every one of mine, even the abysmal failures, you will soon be planning again.

'From our dreams are born the great joys of life. But dreams we must have, and all the time. I prefer dreams to memories.'
Gaston Rebuffat, *Starlight and Storm* (Kaye and Ward 1968)

Further Reading

Books mentioned in the text:

Banks, Mike, *Greenland* (David and Charles 1975)

Baume, Louis, *Sivalaya* (West Col 1978)

Beaud, Philippe, *Peruvian Andes* (Cordee 1988)

Bennet, Donald, *Staunings Alps* (West Col 1972)

Benuzzi, Felice, *No Picnic on Mount Kenya* (William Kimber 1952)

Boardman, Pete, *The Shining Mountain* (Hodder & Stoughton 1978)

Bonington, Chris, *Everest: the Unclimbed Ridge* (W. W. Norton 1983)

Braham, Trevor, *Himalayan Odyssey* (Allen and Unwin 1974)

Bremer-Kamp, Cherie, *Living on the Edge* (David & Charles 1987)

Bruce, Charles, *Himalayan Wanderer* (Alexander Maclehose 1934)

Cleare, John, *Mountains and Mountaineering* (Collins 1979)

Cliff, Peter, *Ski Mountaineering* (Unwin Hyman 1987)

Gunn, Carolyn, *Expedition Cook Book* (Chockstone Press 1988)

Hurn, Martyn, *Skiing Real Snow* (Crowood Press 1987)

Kelsey, Michael, *Guide to the World's Mountains* (Cordee 1987)

Longstaff, Tom, *This My Voyage* (John Murray 1950)

Lopez, Barry, *Arctic Dreams* (Macmillan 1986)

Maraini, Fosco, *Karakoram* (Hutchinson 1961)

Maraini, Fosco, *Where Four Worlds Meet* (Hamish Hamilton 1964)

Mason, Kenneth, *Abode of Snow* (Rupert Hart-Davis 1955)

Messner, Reinhold, *The Seventh Grade* (Kaye and Ward 1974)

Neate, Jill, *Mountaineering in the Andes* (Expedition Advisory Centre 1987)

Ponting, Herbert, *The Great White South* (Duckworth 1921)

Randall, Glen, *Mount McKinley Climber's Handbook* (Genet Expeditions 1984)

Shipton, Eric, *Nanda Devi* (Hodder & Stoughton 1936)

Simpson, Joe, *Touching the Void* (Jonathan Cape 1988)

Tasker, Joe, *Savage Arena* (Methuen 1982)

Thesiger, Wilfred, *Desert, Marsh and Mountains* (Collins 1979)

Tilman, H. W., *China to Chitral* (C.U. Press 1951)

Venables, Stephen, *Painted Mountains* (Hodder & Stoughton 1986)

Ward, Michael, *In This Short Span* (Gollancz 1972)

Wielochowski, Andrew, *East African International Mountain Guide* (West Col 1986)

Wilkerson, James A., *Medicine for Mountaineering* (Mountaineers of Seattle 1985)

Winser, Nigel and Shane, *Expedition Planners Handbook and Directory* (Expedition Advisory Centre, annually)

Articles mentioned in the text:

Boardman, Pete, 'Long Necks in the Hindu Kush', *Mountain 23*

Child, Greg, 'On Broad Peak', *Mountain 94*

Collister, Rob, 'A Summer in Gilgit', *A J 1977*

Collister, Rob, 'Small Expeditions in the Himalaya' *A J 1979*

Collister, Rob, 'A Karakoram Midget', *Climber and Rambler June 1976*

Kurtyka, Voytek, 'The Art of Suffering', *Mountain 121*

Ward, Michael, 'The Mountaineer at Extreme Altitude', *A J 1988–89*

West, John B., 'Oxygenless Climbs and Barometric Pressure', *AAJ 1984*

Other books of interest:

'Comparatively few travellers have visited Chinese Turkestan; which is perhaps just as well because, of those fortunate few, not many have refrained from writing a book.'
> H. W. Tilman, *China to Chitral*

Until quite recently, this remark was true of expedition mountaineering in general, as Tilman himself, with wry humour, would have been the first to acknowledge. Climbers have always been prolific writers. Nowadays, although the number of expedition books being produced has not diminished (on the contrary it seems to increase yearly, as does the number of climbers), most climbers find a readier outlet for their literary talents in one of the many journals and magazines. At all events, there is a vast literature on the subject of expeditions, large and small, all of some interest, but much of it pretty indigestible. This short list is of personal favourites – classics that give a 'feel' for different areas.

Benuzzi, Felice, *No Picnic on Mount Kenya* (William Kimber 1952). Escape from a POW camp to go climbing.

Bowman, W. E., *The Ascent of Rum Doodle* (Parrish 1956). Parody of a large expedition.

Clark, Simon, *The Puma's Claw* (The Adventurers Club 1959). First ascent of Pumasillo in the Cordillera Villacambra, Peru.

Harrer, Heinrich, *Seven Years in Tibet* (Rupert Hart-Davies 1953). Escape from internment in India and subsequent adventures.

Herbert, Wally, *A World of Men* (Eyre & Spottiswoode 1968). Sledging in the Antarctic Peninsula.

Mikkelsen, Ejnar, *Two Against the Ice* (Rupert Hart-Davis 1957). Amazing sledge journeys in N.E. Greenland in the early years of the century.

Newby, Eric, *A Short Walk in the Hindu Kush* (Secker & Warburg 1958). Overland journey and attempt on Mir Samir – often hilariously funny.

Roberts, Dave, *Mountain of My Fear* (Vanguard Press 1968). First ascent of West Face of Huntingdon – a breakthrough in Alaskan climbing – and death of one climber on the descent.

Schaller, George, *Stones of Silence* (André Deutsch 1980). Journeys in Nepal and Chitral in search of the Snow Leopard.

The works of Shipton and Tilman must be required reading for anyone interested in small expeditions, their mastery of the written word, albeit expressed in very different styles, matching their mastery of lightweight mountain travel. Diadem has recently published their collected works, Shipton's in one volume, Tilman's in two – bargains, all of them!

Appendix

Useful Addresses

British Mountaineering Council
Crawford House
Precinct Centre
Booth St East
Manchester M13 9RZ
Tel: 061 273 5835

Expedition Advisory Centre
Royal Geographical Society
Kensington Gore
London SW7 2AR
Tel: 01 581 2057

American Alpine Club
113 East 90th St
New York
NY 10128-1589
Tel: 212-722 1628

American Mountain Foundation
121 E. Espanola
Colorado Springs
Colorado 80907
Tel: 719-471 8418

Reference Libraries

Britain

Alpine Club
74 South Audley St
London W1Y 5FF
(This address will be changing at some time
in 1989.)
Tel: 01 499 1542

Royal Geographical Society
1 Kensington Gore
London SW7 2AR
Tel: 01 581 2057
(The Map Room is open to the public but the
library is restricted to Fellows of the
Society.)

Al Rouse Memorial Library
Sheffield City Library

Graham Brown Memorial Library
Scottish National Library
Edinburgh

USA

The American Alpine Club library has a
number of different branches, namely:

New York – 113E 90th St, New York

Rocky Mountain – Rare Books Room,
Norlin Library, University of Colorado,
Boulder

Seattle – The Mountaineers Library, 300 3rd
Avenue, Seattle

Sierra Nevada – Yosemite Research Library

South California – Malibu County Library

Teton – Teton County Library, Jackson,
Wyoming

Information on climbing and travel books currently in print can be obtained from:

Cordee
3a De Montfort Street
Leicester LE1 7HD
Tel: 0533 543 579

For maps, contact:
Stanfords
10 Long Acre
London WC2

Addresses for Permission

These do change so it is usually worth contacting the embassy concerned first. In the case of Pakistan and India this is the quickest and surest way of obtaining a copy of the Rules and Regulations and an application form. For Nepal and Bhutan it is better to write direct.

His Majesty's Government
Mountaineering Expedition Section
Ministry of Tourism
Kalmati
Kathmandu
Nepal

For trekking peaks in Nepal:
Nepalese Mountaineering Association
Sports Council Building
16/53 Ram Shah Path
P.O. Box 1435
Kathmandu
Nepal

Government of Pakistan
Ministry of Culture and Tourism
Islamabad
Pakistan

Indian Mountaineering Foundation
Anand Niketan Road
Nr. Ram Land Anand College
New Delhi 110–021

Bhutan Tourism Corporation
P.O. Box 159
Thimphu
Bhutan

Chinese Mountaineering Association
All China Sports Federation
9 Tiyuguan Road
Beijing
People's Republic of China

Ministry for Greenland
3 Hausergade
DK–1128 Copenhagen K
Denmark

McKinley National Park
P.O. Box 9
McKinley Park
Alaska 99755

Sovalptour
V/O Sovintersport
Boljshoi
Rzevskij
Pereulok
5 Moscow 121069
USSR

Addresses for Grants

The Mount Everest Foundation and the BMC are the two main bodies providing financial support to mountaineering expeditions.

Having identified your objective(s), write

to the MEF for details of eligibility and for application forms:

MEF
Hon. Secretary Bill Ruthven
Gowrie
Cardwell Close
Warton
Preston PR4 1SH
Tel: 0772 635346

Applications to the BMC are made via the MEF using the same application form and the same interviewing procedure.

It is not necessary to have permission from the country concerned before applying to the MEF, although it is wise to apply for permission as early as possible so that it is definitely granted before the expedition leaves Britain. The closing dates for applications to the MEF are 31 August and 31 December. These are strictly adhered to so it is necessary to think well in advance. For example, applications must be in before the year end at the latest for any expedition the following year.

Other Awards

Nick Estcourt Award
Secretary
24 Grange Road
Bowden
Cheshire WA14 3EE

A single grant is made each year to a team planning a significant lightweight expedition. Closing date 30 November each year.

Alison Chadwick Memorial Fund
Secretary ACMF
'Oakland'
Trevanion Road
Wadebridge
Cornwall PL27 7NZ

This award exists to provide financial assistance to women participating in expeditionary mountaineering among the 'Greater Ranges'.

Mick Burke Award
Ned Kelly
Natural History Unit
British Broadcasting Corporation
Whiteladies Road
Bristol 8

This award, administered by the BBC, is for expedition filming.

Insurance

Insurance brokers who will quote for expeditions:

Insurance Dept.
BMC Services Ltd
Crawford House
Precinct Centre
Booth Street East
Manchester M13 9RZ
Tel: 061 273 5839

Alexander Stenhouse Ltd
Richmond House
College Street
Southampton SO9 4ZB
Tel: 0703 225616

West Mercia Insurance Services
High Street
Wombourne
Near Wolverhampton WV5 9DN
Tel: 0902 892661

Cambell Irvine Ltd
48 Earls Court Road
London W8 6EJ
Tel: 01 937 6981

Mountain First Aid Courses

Plas y Brenin
Capel Curig
Betws y Coed
Gwynedd

Wilderness and Expedition Skills Training
Arrina
Shieldaig
Strathcarron
Ross-shire

Air Taxis in the Alaska Range

K2 Aviation
P.O. Box 290
Talkeetna
AK 99676

Doug Geeting Aviation
P.O. Box 42
Talkeetna
AK 99676

Talkeetna Air Taxi
P.O. Box 73
Talkeetna
AK 99676

Dog Team Operators in Alaska

Denali Dog Tours
P.O. Box 1
McKinley Park AK 99755

Bob Crockett
P.O. Box 261
Girdwood/Alyeska AK 99587

Alaskan Treks
P.O. Box 82655
Fairbanks AK 99708

Index